What Saying About This Book?

Dr. Stanley Hibbs, in his latest book, [...] has tackled one of life's most universal perplexing problems in a practical down-to-earth way that will give every reader fresh insight and guidance. I predict that Dr Hibbs' book will become a must have, well-thumbed, much consulted classic guidebook which every minister, coach, mentor or therapist will use with their congregations, mentees, clients and patients.

- Rev. Dr. John Lutwyche Clements, author, international speaker and life coach

Great self-help advice for people who fight procrastination in their lives. Full of tips and exercises, this short book makes the daunting task seem less challenging, even simple. I personally found it very helpful.

- Tak Keung Sin, office worker

Consider It Done!

Ten Prescriptions for Finishing What you Start

Stanley E. Hibbs, Ph.D.

Second Edition

Multi-Media Publications Inc.

Oshawa, Ontario

Consider It Done!
By Stanley E. Hibbs, Ph.D.

Managing Editor: Kevin Aguanno
Typesetting: Charles Sin
Cover Design: Troy O'Brien

Published by:
Multi-Media Publications Inc.
Box 58043, Rosslynn RPO, Oshawa, Ontario, Canada, L1J 8L6

http://www.mmpubs.com/

ISBN (Paperback):   1-897326-51-3 / 9781897326510
ISBN (Adobe PDF eBook):   1-897326-72-6 / 9781897326725
ISBN (Mobipocket PRC eBook):   1-897326-73-4 / 9781897326732
ISBN (Microsoft LIT eBook):   1-897326-74-2 / 9781897326749

Published in Canada. Printed simultaneously in U.S.A. and England.

CIP Data available from the publisher.

First edition published October 2004 by iUniverse as ISBN 0-595-32822-9.

Contents

Preface

I suspect that every writer wants to impress his readers. I'm really no different, but I don't want you to be impressed with *me*. I want you to be impressed with *yourself*. I want you to have greater confidence in your God-given abilities. One way to have that greater confidence is to take on any long-term project and see it through to the end.

That is what this book is all about.

It doesn't matter what project you take on, as long as it's consistent with your moral principles and fulfills some worthwhile purpose in your life or the lives of others. You may want to stop smoking, lose weight, build a successful business, or train for the Olympics. Whatever your goal, the principles in this book can help you to finish what you start.

In the development of this book, I owe much to the writings of numerous psychologists and specialists in the area of human productivity and performance. As a psychologist, teacher, and personal Coach, my professional life has been devoted to the study, application, and teaching of these principles. I have seen many lives significantly improved by the consistent application of these ideas.

There are other self-help books that deal with motivation, goal setting, time management and the other concepts covered in this book. However, I believe that this book stands out for several reasons:

1. This book is an easy read. I've taken volumes of material and distilled then into a simple step-by-step process.

2. I have included user-friendly charts that allow you interact with this material, not just read it.

3. Many chapters contain a Coach's Corner that gives concrete examples of how these principles can work for you.

The greatest joy of being a therapist is seeing how people make positive changes. Their problems are different, but the process of change is remarkably similar. The principles that help someone overcome depression and anxiety are the same principles that help someone stop smoking, develop more self-confidence, manage time effectively, overcome procrastination, and successfully complete any long-term project.

Although people usually seek psychotherapy at times of distress, they often see it as a surprisingly positive experience. Oddly enough, some clients are even grateful for the problems that drove them to therapy in the first place. I think this is because therapy helped them learn to apply the principles of change.

It hardly seems fair that only therapy patients get the benefits of therapy. Do you have to be depressed, anxious, or at the end of your rope to want to change and grow? I think not. So, it became my mission to introduce positive change strategies to a larger audience.

My first step was to become trained as a personal and executive Coach. Since coaching is often done by phone, my work is no longer limited to those able to fight Atlanta's legendary traffic to get to my office. I can work with the graduate student in California, the business owner in Virginia, and the attorney on Manhattan.

The second step has been to develop seminars and workshops. I have presented my "Consider It Done" seminars to civic, corporate, and religious organizations. Some of these seminars have been in-person while others have been via teleconference. Topics have included "Overcoming Procrastination" and "Jump Start Your Week."

This book is my latest effort to reach out to a wider audience. In the past, I didn't believe that I could write a book. However, as I shared my Ten Prescriptions with my clients, they encouraged me to put these ideas in writing. Obviously, once I told people that I was writing a book about *finishing what you start*, I had to finish it!

Today, I'm a "recovering procrastinator" who consciously strives to apply these principles on a daily basis. My greatest hope is that I will give you faith that if I can do it, you can too!

Important Notes

- The stories included in this book are composites designed to underscore important points and show the *Consider It Done!* principles in action. Any resemblance to a single person or situation is purely coincidental.

- This book contains a number of tables and checklists for you to complete as you work through the Ten Prescriptions. If you are reading an electronic copy (e-book version), you may wish to print your copy of the book in order to complete these tables and checklists.

- You may refer to this book numerous times to complete different Behavior Change Projects.

- Every word in this book is designed to help you be a happier and more successful person. I have no intention of getting you "psyched up" or turning you into something that you are not. If anything that I've written puts undue pressure on you or makes you feel displeased with yourself, I will not have served you well. However, please forgive me if I point out a way in which you may already be displeased with yourself.

1

The Agonizing Gap

Before we get too far into the material in this book, I'd like to start off with a simple question: can you hear yourself making any of these statements?

> "I started out great on my diet, but I didn't last a week!"

> "I know that I could dramatically increase my sales volume if I made more cold calls, but I can't make myself do them."

> "I bought an exercise bike that I never use."

> "My doctor tells me that I need a regular program of exercise. I know he's right, but I can't make myself do it."

> "I hate cigarettes, but I can't give them up."

> "There just isn't enough time to do all the things that I'd like to do."

"I really want to change careers, but it's easier to stay where I am."

"I regret never getting my college degree, but I couldn't possibly do it now."

"It would be great to go into business for myself, but I'm scared to try."

Did you notice yourself wincing or feeling a knot in your stomach as you read these statements? If so, don't feel bad. It only means that you're human. Most of us are aware of what I call the "agonizing gap" between what we desire to accomplish in life and what we actually do accomplish.

Most of us have given up on a diet. Most of us have vowed to watch less TV and read more. Most of us desire to have more time with family and friends, only to get swamped by the minutia of life. Many of us have a dream that has remained unfulfilled for such a long time that it's become painful to think about.

So if everyone has this gap, where does the pain come from? The pain is entirely self-inflicted. It's caused by our own tendency to mentally berate ourselves for not living up to our own expectations.

Depending on your personal religious tradition, you may or may not recognize this quote: "I do not understand what I do. For what I want to do, I do not do, but what I hate, I do."

Every faith tradition has its own heroes, people we admire for the good they did. Those of you with a Christian background may recognize the author of these lines as the Apostle Paul. The quote comes straight from the book of Romans in the *New Testament* (Romans 7:15).

Paul was a very energetic, focused, and productive man. He made long journeys by foot and established churches throughout what are now Turkey and Greece. He wrote long letters to his followers in which he outlined the basic tenants of the new faith. He was thrown in jail, beaten, stoned, shipwrecked, and even bitten by a poisonous snake. None of this kept him from getting a lot of things done. Yet notice how hard he was on himself.

So if even saints are aware of falling short, maybe you can forgive yourself for not accomplishing all that you have hoped.

Being excessively self-critical will not help you move ahead. Yes, you have tried to quit smoking before and didn't. Yes, you have vowed to be more productive only to slip back into your old bad habits. So what? Your past failures and setbacks do not have to dictate your future...and though you may have heard this before, I intend to help you truly believe it.

As you begin the process described in this book, let me suggest the following attitudes:

1. Be skeptical but not cynical.

2. Allow yourself a little bit of hope and faith.

3. Strive for excellence, but be gentle and kind with yourself when you fall short.

How to Best Use This Book

You have a choice about how you read this book. You can read it through quickly to get the overall idea. It's perfectly all right to use the book this way.

However, an abstract understanding of general principles will only take you so far. So I recommend that you use this book to start your own Behavior Change Project. This way, my suggestions won't just be abstract ideas, but rather practical tools that you can actually experience in action.

What is a Behavior Change Project? It's any project that, once completed, helps you be more productive, successful, and balanced...any endeavor that helps you feel better about yourself and improves your relationships with others.

There are two types of Behavior Change Projects: Linear Projects and Habit Change Projects.

Linear Projects

I call some Projects "Linear" because they have a beginning, middle, and a specific end point. A Linear Project may involve the fulfillment of a major life dream. The Project may involve the development of a particular product (e.g., a book, invention, or work of art), the acquisition of a certain skill (e.g., playing the guitar), or the attainment of a certain position in life (e.g., earning a degree, succeeding in your own business). It may be something we intend to do only once.

Here are some examples of Linear Projects:

- Finishing your college degree

- Completing your graduate thesis or dissertation

- Building your home-based business to a profitable level

- Completing a major home renovation

- Going through a major job search

- Making a significant career change

- Developing your own web site

- Inventing and marketing a new product

- Becoming competent on the computer

- Learning a martial art

- Learning a foreign language

- Founding a nonprofit organization

- Opening a school

- Developing a comprehensive financial plan

- Learning to play a musical instrument

- Hiking the Rocky Mountains or the Appalachian Trail

- Writing a book

- Designing and building a new home

- Getting rid of years of household clutter

- Developing a new software program

The possibilities are endless. Is there any long-term dream that you have deferred for too long? Maybe it's time to get started.

Habit Change Projects

Habit Change Projects involve a lifestyle change and/or the development of a new positive habit. The goal is not to develop a specific product or skill, but a new pattern of behavior. Unlike Linear Projects, Habit Change Projects have no specific end point. Success is measured by how well the new habit is established.

Here are some examples of Habit Change Projects:

- Regular exercise

- Quality reading

- Management of a health condition such as diabetes or high blood pressure

- Becoming more punctual

- Increasing cold calls to potential customers

- Keeping the checkbook balanced

- Timely filing of expense reports or taxes

- Staying on top of housework

- Managing paperwork

- Keeping promises

- Spending time in prayer and meditation

- Doing all tasks in a more timely and efficient manner

All the Projects listed above involve the establishment of a desired habit. However, sometimes a Habit Change Project zeroes in on a habit you wish to eliminate.

Here are some examples:

- Smoking
- Excessive drinking
- Watching too much TV
- Procrastinating
- Losing your temper

A note of caution with respect to Habit Change Projects: Because of the potential negative consequence of some harmful habits (e.g., excessive drinking), you should not attempt to tackle these problems armed only with this book. If you want to take on one of these habits, I urge you to consult a qualified mental health provider. This book can be helpful, but must not be seen as a substitute for competent treatment.

Other negative habits (e.g., procrastination) are just the "flip side" of more positive habits. For example, rather than have a project to "eliminate procrastination," I would advise you to embark on a project to "complete all tasks in a more timely and efficient manner."

In fact, for any goal setting you do, it is best to state a goal in positive terms. This is because we think in terms of pictures, and we cannot "see" the word *not*. So if I tell you *not* to think of a pink elephant, what do you immediately see? Likewise, if you hand a cup of water to your toddler and say, "Don't spill it," what picture does the child have? That's right; the child sees "spill," which tells him what *not* to do, but doesn't tell him what he's supposed to do. It's much better to say, "Hold this cup carefully with both hands so all of the water will stay in the cup."

How Many?

You may be wondering, "Is it okay to tackle more than one Behavior Change Project at a time?" Yes, but do not spread yourself too thin. If you are undertaking a major Linear Project such as writing a book or making a major career transition, that may be all you can do. Certainly you can't expect yourself to develop a multimillion dollar company, write a book, hike the Appalachian Trail, and learn the flute all at one time.

Sometimes Habit Change Projects can help you complete a Linear Project. For example, in the process of writing this book (a Linear Project), I had to make progress on several Habit Change Projects such as "more effective planning and time management." If you have a Linear Project to "build a business," it might be very helpful to establish the habit of "increasing cold calls to potential customers."

I invite you to stop now and think about what type of Project you want to tackle. Be sure to write it down, either in the space below or on a separate sheet of paper.

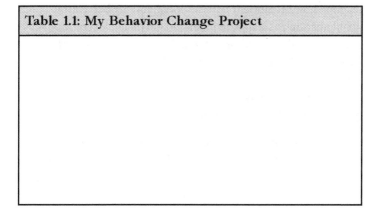

Table 1.1: My Behavior Change Project

A Coach Can Help

If you have decided to take on a Behavior Change Project, I hope you're excited and eager to get started. However, if you're like most people, you may also be a little nervous. You may be already telling yourself that you'll never finish. That is a very normal reaction, but it doesn't have to hold you back.

If you think it's going to be tough, I strongly suggest that you get a Coach.

What is a Coach? A good definition was given to me by Dr. Ben Dean, Executive Director of MentorCoach, an organization that trains licensed therapists to become Coaches. Dr. Dean's definition of a Coach is "someone who helps you get clear on your most important goals, then helps you craft a plan to reach those goals, then walks with you while you take the action steps necessary to reach those goals. It's like having a silent business partner who is totally committed to your success, but you keep the profits."

People often ask how coaching is different from psychotherapy. Although the two services overlap, there are some important differences. Psychotherapy focuses on the diagnosis and treatment of emotional and/or behavioral problems such as depression and anxiety. The client may be emotionally distressed or vulnerable at the beginning of treatment. Because of this, psychotherapy should only be provided by a licensed mental health professional such as a psychologist or licensed clinical social worker. Most psycho-therapy is conducted in person.

Coaching focuses more on helping the client reach desired levels of effectiveness, productivity, and life balance. The client will not be distressed at the outset. Although some Coaches are also mental health professionals, many have backgrounds in business, education, or other professions. Coaching is usually conducted by phone and/or e-mail.

Common coaching issues include career satisfaction, effective goal setting, leadership skill development, and time management.

Where can you find a coach? I am familiar with two coach referral services. MentorCoach specializes in training mental health professions to become coaches. You can expect their graduates to be first-rate (www.mentorcoach.com). For those for coaching from a particularly Christian perspective, the Christian Coaches Network (www.christiancoaches.com) is a good option.

If you're unable to use the services of a Coach because of a limited budget, you can still apply the principles in this book to help you reach your goals. Although you and I may never meet in person, feel free to think of me as your Coach. To help you get a feel for how coaching works, I've included a Coach's Corner in a number of Chapters. Many include examples of exchanges between a Coach and client that are designed to help you understand and apply the Chapter content.

Getting Started

Are you ready to get going? If you feel a solid commitment to your Behavior Change Project and have a moderate level of confidence in your ability to make significant progress, skip to Chapter 5 which describes the first of my Ten Prescriptions. Then, work through the balance of the book.

However, if you need more preparation before you start, read the next three Chapters. In Chapter 2, you will be introduced to the basic principles of Cognitive Therapy and learn that your level of effectiveness is determined by how you think. Chapter 3 is devoted time management. In Chapter 4, you will be given information to help you decide if you're truly ready to get started.

2

You Are What
You Think

Modern psychology has confirmed what many wise people have known for years. Events do not determine what we feel. It's our thoughts about events. By "thoughts" I mean our interpretations, beliefs, expectations, opinions, and attitudes.

Our thoughts are often so automatic that we don't pay attention to them. We just react. However, when we pay attention to our thinking, we can often change it, and thus change how we feel. Let's look at an example:

Mike is in deep trouble. He was rushing to an important job interview when he got caught in traffic. His cell phone battery is dead, so he has no way to reach his prospective employer. He desperately needs this job because he has a wife and two kids to support. He is extremely upset. His heart is pounding and he is having trouble concentrating on his driving. His face is turning red and perspiration is soaking through his shirt. He is just about as miserable as a man can be.

By sheer coincidence, Carl, who is stuck in the same traffic jam, is also late for a job interview. He has been out of work for as long as Mike, and his financial needs are essentially the same. His daughter borrowed his cell phone the day before, so he also has no way of contacting his prospective employer. However, Carl is handling it differently. Not that he is happy; it's not a situation in which you would expect any rational person to be happy. However, he is remaining calm and trying to figure out what to do.

What makes Mike and Carl so different? Why is one of them utterly stressed out while the other is making the best of it? There are a number of possible explanations, all potentially valid: genetics, brain chemistry, temperament, parental modeling, early childhood experiences, and many others. However, when we look closely at the difference, it all boils down to a difference in thinking.

If we could monitor Mike's thinking, it would be something like, "This is horrible. I'm such a loser. Here's a chance for a great job, and I mess it up. Things like this always happen to me. They'll think I'm not fit if I'm late. I'll never get the job now. I may never get another job. My wife will be very upset with me. I should have remembered to charge my cell phone battery. I'm so lazy and irresponsible."

Carl's situation is identical, but his thinking is very different: "This is a pretty bad problem. Next time, I'll have to start a little sooner. They may be displeased with me for being late, but I'll just tell them what happened. Maybe they'll overlook it and give me the job anyway. If not, I'll just try harder to get the next one. I need to take a few deep breaths and calm down. I'll get there as soon as I can."

The good news is that Mike can learn to think more like Carl. Cognitive Therapy is an approach to treatment that would be ideal for Mike. He would learn that thoughts like "I'm such a loser" only serve to make a bad situation worse. His overly negative thoughts would be replaced with thoughts that are more realistic and situation-specific. He'd still have unpleasant feelings, but he would not be a victim of these feelings. He would realize he has the option to think the old way and feel miserable or to think in new ways and feel better. It takes a lot of effort, but I have seen many depressed and anxious clients turn their lives around by using these techniques.

I am telling you all of this because a key to success in your Behavior Change Project will be your ability to manage your mood. You will get discouraged. You may have feelings of self-doubt and inadequacy. You may struggle with anxiety and worry. But when you learn how to manage your mood, there will be no stopping you. So let's learn more about where your bad moods come from.

27

Meet Your Gremlin

We all have certain negative habits of thinking. Let's say you have just been given a big promotion at work. Along with your higher salary, you will be given some added responsibility. You're excited at first, but the night before you start, you wake up in the middle of the night. Your head is filled with thoughts like, "What if I can't do it? Maybe I shouldn't have agreed to take it. My co-workers will resent me for the promotion. I've done okay so far, but eventually they'll see that I can't handle it."

That, my friend, is your Gremlin speaking.

The Gremlin represents all of the negative thoughts that attack us any time we step out to try something new. It is the source of much of our self-doubt, excessive guilt, and irrational anxiety. If you're not where you want to be in life, there's a good chance your Gremlin is part of the reason.

Where does the Gremlin come from? No matter how fortunate we have been, we have all experienced loss, rejection, embarrassment, frustration, and humiliation. We can't escape them; they are part of being alive. We didn't make the team, we were turned down for a date, someone laughed at us, or we did something embarrassing. Even our best friends sometimes say hurtful things. From these experiences, we learn to doubt ourselves. Because it hurts to fail, we don't want to try anything risky. Because it hurts to be rejected, we don't reach out to develop new relationships.

Not that the Gremlin is all bad. It does serve a purpose. Sometimes it's healthy to be pessimistic. If I only had positive thoughts, I wouldn't see the dentist twice a year or get my annual medical check up. I wouldn't file my taxes on time or buy professional liability insurance. A little guilt, self-doubt, and worry are helpful.

But too often, the Gremlin is there to rob us of our hope, enthusiasm, and even our self-worth. You can't eliminate the Gremlin, but you can outsmart it by learning to dispute its negative thinking.

Coach's Corner

In our first Coach's Corner, we will see how Marsha's Coach helps her stop being so hard on herself by refuting the negative messages coming from her Gremlin.

Marsha: "I'm so disgusted with myself this week!"

Coach: "What happened?"

Marsha: "Nothing, that's the problem. I didn't do any work at all on my dissertation. I know that I should just shake it off, but I'm beating myself up about it. I'm beginning to think that I'm just not Ph.D. material."

Coach: "Would it be okay if we explored some ways to work through this?"

Marsha: "Please, I need that."

Coach: "Maybe we could start by taking a look at what you just said to me. You're beginning to think that you're not 'Ph.D. material.' Exactly what do you mean by 'Ph.D. material?'"

Marsha: "Someone who is 'Ph.D. material' would be intelligent and possess the self-discipline to do the work that needs to be done."

Coach: "Do you have any intelligence and self-discipline, or are you totally lacking in these qualities?"

Marsha: "Well, I did well in undergraduate school, I tested well, and I was accepted into graduate school, so I guess that I have the basic intelligence. I think that self-discipline is my biggest problem."

Coach: "Okay, how about self-discipline? Are you completely lacking in that? Are you totally out of control?"

Marsha: "No, I've got some self-discipline. On some days, I do pretty well."

Coach: "So self-discipline is something that can change from day to day?"

Marsha: "Right."

Coach: "So if it changes from day to day, then it might be something that can improve with effort and practice?"

Marsha: "Yes, but what if I can't develop enough self-discipline in time to get the dissertation done by the deadline?"

Coach: "I'll be happy to explore that question with you. But first, do you remember what we said about the Gremlin?"

Marsha: "You said that when I start anything new, I'd have a lot of negative self-talk. I'd get discouraged."

Coach: "Right, I also said that you would give yourself a lot of negative labels such as 'lazy' or 'stupid.' Could that be what's happening here?"

Marsha: "I suppose so. What do I do about it?"

Coach: "Great question. What do you do with any negative self-talk?"

Marsha: "Explore it, find out where it's distorted, and create some alternative ways of thinking."

Coach: "Exactly. Are you ready to take on the Gremlin?"

Marsha: "Okay, you told me that I would experience the Gremlin any time I took on anything new."

Coach: "Right. So in some ways, hearing the Gremlin speak is a good sign. It means you're taking on something new. The only way to completely avoid the Gremlin is to never try anything."

Marsha: "Well, even that wouldn't work for me, because then I would condemn myself for not trying."

Coach: "So whatever you do, the Gremlin is going to speak. In that case, you might as well take him on. Remember, what is the Gremlin?"

Marsha: "It's my own negative thoughts."

Coach: "So if they're your thoughts, who can change them?"

Marsha: "Me."

Marsha's Gremlin is a fairly common one. The problem is not her intelligence or self-discipline. The problem is that her Gremlin is causing her to doubt herself, which takes away much of the energy she needs to get the job done. As she learns how to outsmart her Gremlin by refuting the negative self-talk, she will start making progress on her dissertation.

Here's a radical suggestion: Next time you start to feel discouraged, recognize it as your Gremlin. See your discouragement as a positive sign because it means that you're trying something new and attempting to make a positive change in your life.

In the space below, write three to five negative thoughts you have whenever you try something new or tackle a big project (e.g., "I can't do that," "I'll never finish," "I remember the last time I tried to make a change like that…").

Table 2.1: My Gremlin is talking when I am thinking...
1.
2.
3.
4.
5.

Now that you've met your Gremlin, you must take responsibility for overcoming it. If you're the type of person who often feels overwhelmed and powerless in taking control of your life, the following section may help.

Proactive vs. Reactive Living

In Steven Covey's classic book, *The Seven Habits of Highly Effective People* (Simon & Schuster, 1989), habit number one is "Be proactive." Since the book was published, the term "proactive" has become part of our culture. It sounds good, but what does it really mean?

Here's how I think of it. I imagine a line. On one end, I write the words *Proactive*, *Intentional*, and *Takes Responsibility*. On the other end, I write *Reactive*, *Unintentional*, and *Avoids Responsibility*.

In any given moment, we are all somewhere on this line. Sometimes we're on the Proactive end, sometimes the Reactive. However, most often we're somewhere in the middle.

People living at the Proactive end operate according to their principles, not their moods. They make plans and follow them. They set goals, and their daily habits are directed toward reaching those goals. Proactive people plan their month/week/day and follow their plan as much as possible.

Proactive people assume responsibility for their actions, choices, and even their moods. They are not victims of circumstances, other people, or their own temperament. If they have planned to do something, they will do it even if they don't "feel" like doing it. Needless to say, proactive people get more things done, enjoy life more, and generally feel pretty good about themselves and other people.

People who spend most of their time on the Reactive end rarely have goals or plan anything with any intent to follow through. They may feel like a pinball, bouncing from one action to the next without any sense of direction. They react to situations based on their moods, not their principles. They often feel like victims of their circumstances, other people, or their own weaknesses. Rather than assume responsibility for their lives, they blame others or wallow in self-pity.

People on the Reactive end are less likely to be productive or happy, or to experience genuine self-worth.

On the next page is an example of the difference.

See the difference? My suggestion is that from time to time, you ask yourself where you are on the spectrum. If you have been floundering around and not getting much done, chances are you're down at the Reactive end. If you are, make a conscious decision to move toward the Proactive end. It's not easy at first, but with practice you'll be able to do it. You'll be amazed at how much progress you'll make simply by moving even slightly toward the Proactive end.

A proactive person has decided to start attending church services on Sunday morning. She firmly commits to it. She reinforces this commitment by marking it on her calendar and telling others of her plans.

All week long, she knows what she will do Sunday morning. Since she may need to get up early Sunday morning, she makes a point of not staying up too late Saturday night. She gets her clothes ready the night before and sets her alarm. In other words, all her actions are consistent with her intention to go to church. Barring some emergency, she'll be there.

A reactive person in the same scenario might think it would be a good idea to go to church "someday." On Saturday, she tells herself, "Maybe I'll go tomorrow. I'll see how I feel in the morning." She stays up late Saturday night and neglects to set the alarm. She still wakes up early enough but tells herself, "I don't have enough time to get ready." Feeling guilty and yet a little relieved, she goes back to sleep.

Here's an exercise: Think of a time when you were on the Reactive end. Maybe you wasted a lot of time. Maybe you felt unorganized. Maybe you felt like you were spinning your wheels. What were you doing at that time? What challenges were you facing? What feelings did you have about your circumstances? How did you feel about yourself? In the space below, write a description of what this time was like for you.

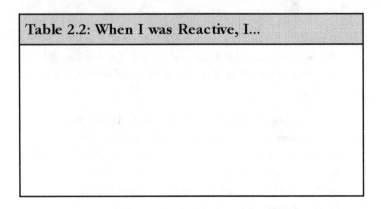

Think of a time when you were Proactive. You used your time efficiently. You felt organized and you accomplished what you set out to do. What were you doing? What factors might have contributed to your focus and productivity? In the space below, write down what that was like for you.

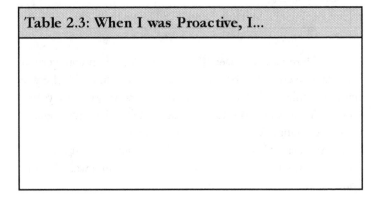

Remember, when you notice yourself on the Reactive end, you can make a conscious decision to move toward the Proactive end.

3

Powerful Time Management

Hint: Put the big rocks in first.

If thinking about your Behavior Change Project triggers some uncomfortable feelings, let me suggest one culprit: time! Time is the Gremlin's greatest ally.

We tell ourselves that we don't have the time to finish what we start, so there is no point in starting. We know that we often waste time, so we focus on what we haven't done rather than on what we could do in the future. We are painfully aware that there is only so much time in a day, a week, a year, and our lives. Time anxiety can be crippling. If time flows on like a river, it's easy to feel like we're being carried along with the rapids, totally out of control and headed for Niagara Falls.

Many of us whine and complain about time…"I have too much to do. There's not enough time in the day. I'm always rushing here and there." There's an element of anger and blame in these statements, as if it's someone else's fault that we don't use our time effectively. This is understandable, but this attitude won't get you where you want to go.

I'm a self-confessed time waster myself. I turn on my computer, and my first impulse is to play a game. I start to do some professional reading, but the most recent *People* magazine catches my eye. I need to reorganize my office, but there's always tomorrow. My Gremlin gets me both ways. It gives me excuses for wasting my time, and then it berates me when I do.

It's helpful to realize that time doesn't play favorites. We all have the same 24 hours. Bill Gates, Ted Turner, and the President get no more hours in the day than you do. The person who lies in bed all day also has the same amount of time. It's how we use it that matters.

To manage time most effectively, we must think along the Proactive versus Reactive dimension I discussed in Chapter 2. How does a proactive person manage time? He thinks about what he needs to do, plans a schedule, and follows the schedule as closely as he can. Planning and follow through are essential to his effectiveness.

The Four Quadrants

So how do we plan? Again, I turn to Steven Covey for a useful system to help organize and manage my time. The diagram below illustrates his famous four-quadrant model of time management.

	Urgent	Not Urgent
Important	1	2
Not Important	3	4

Figure 3.1 - From The Seven Habits of Highly Effective People, © *1989 Stephen R. Covey. Reprinted with permission. All rights reserved.*

Importance

(The following is drawn from The Seven Habits of Highly Effective People, *© 1989 Stephen R. Covey. Reprinted with permission. All rights reserved.)*

In choosing how to invest our time, Covey asks us to categorize all activities as either Important or Unimportant. To decide whether an activity is Important, ask yourself:

1. Does this activity help me fulfill an important role in my life (e.g., spouse, parent, worker, business owner, or citizen)?

2. Will this activity move me closer to some significant goal?

3. Does this activity enhance my personal growth and make me a better person?

By these criteria, many people might consider the following activities Important:

1. Work responsibilities

2. Quality time with family

3. Exercise

4. Quality reading and other self-improvement activities

These same people are likely to consider these activities pleasurable but Unimportant:

1. Watching TV

2. Reading junk mail

3. Surfing the Internet

4. Attending sports events

We might enjoy these activities, but they probably don't add much value to our lives, nor do they help us change and grow.

It's tempting to generalize the Important tasks as "work" and the Unimportant as "play," but this is not an accurate distinction. Having lunch with your spouse, watching your son's soccer game, or attending your daughter's Girl Scout meeting are important to anyone who values family. On the other hand, a lot of what passes for work (routine paperwork, excessively long meetings) may not be important at all.

Naturally, there are degrees of importance, so it may not always be easy to categorize all activities neatly into just two boxes. Nevertheless, it makes sense that the more time you spent doing important things, the more effective you will be. You are likely to be happier and more productive than someone who spends the bulk of his time doing things that are unimportant.

Urgency

(The following is drawn from The Seven Habits of Highly Effective People, © *1989 Stephen R. Covey. Reprinted with permission. All rights reserved.)*

The second dimension of Covey's Four Quadrant model concerns an activity's degree of Urgency. An Urgent activity is something for which there is a specific deadline approaching in the near future.

For most of us, getting to work is urgent because we are expected to show up at a specific time. In my own work, all my clinical and coaching appointments are urgent because they are scheduled for a specific day and time. A good part of our time is spent responding to urgent, time-limited demands: The report is due tomorrow; the kids have to be at school at 8:15 AM; we must file our tax returns by April 15.

The Quadrants

(The following is drawn from The Seven Habits of Highly Effective People, *© 1989 Stephen R. Covey. Reprinted with permission. All rights reserved.)*

Let's look at each of the four Quadrants. Much of our work day is devoted to Quadrant 1 (Urgent/Important). We have customers we must please in a timely manner; we have bosses to whom we must report in a timely manner; and we have the stockholders who are expecting the quarterly report any day now. Much of our time is devoted to responding to the demands of the moment.

Let's skip Quadrant 2 (Not Urgent/Important) for a moment and review Quadrant 3 (Urgent/Unimportant) and Quadrant 4 (Not Urgent/Unimportant). These are unimportant activities, whether or not they have a clear deadline. Quadrant 3 consists of activities that require an immediate response, but are of little importance. Returning meaningless phone calls or feeling like you "must" open the useless junk mail before doing other work are examples. Quadrant 4 is easy to define: it's all those things that are neither urgent nor important. Most TV watching, computer games, and "just hanging out" fit into this category.

We return now to Quadrant 2: (Not Urgent/Important). These are activities that would make your life better, improve your relationships, bring you more success, and increase your income. In her book, *Your Best Year Yet* (Warner Books, 2000), Jinny Ditzler refers to Quadrant 2 as "Golden Time" because it's literally the time that could make the biggest difference in our lives.

There's only one problem. Quadrant 2 activities have no looming deadline. There is no teacher waiting for a term paper or boss looking for a financial report. In fact, you never have to do a Quadrant 2 activity if you don't want to.

With no deadline ahead, our natural tendency is to put these activities off until we "have time." The problem is we never "have time" because there is always something that we think is urgent. As Covey says, we tend to let the important be "squeezed out" by the urgent. Covey and others have noticed that most of us spend far too much time reacting to "urgent" things and far too little time on Quadrant 2 activities. Success comes as we gradually increase the amount of time we spend on Quadrant 2 activities.

The secret to increasing the time we spend on Quadrant 2 activities comes in periodic planning, usually at monthly and weekly intervals. Personally, I like to take some time every Sunday night to plan the week ahead (this planning time is itself a Quadrant 2 activity!).

I think about my major roles and goals (e.g., husband, father, Coach, psychologist, etc.). What activities will help me move ahead in reaching those goals? If there is no deadline for a particular activity, I know that I must schedule it in advance. I must "nail" it into my schedule first and make a commitment to engage in that activity at the designated time.

The writing of this book was a Quadrant 2 activity. It was very important to me, but I had no contract to fulfill or publishing deadline to meet. I could have gone on forever and never finished it. So to get it finished, I had to schedule times to write in advance.

I wanted these writing sessions to be as sacred to me as my clinical and coaching sessions, so I came up with an idea. My computer monitor had the brand name *Athena*, so I recorded regular appointments with "Ms. Athena" in my appointment book. Having made a commitment to meet with "Ms. Athena," I was much more likely to keep my appointment.

Filling the Bucket

Let's say you have one empty bucket, one filled with large rocks, one filled with pebbles, and one filled with sand. Your task is to get as much "stuff" into the empty bucket as you can. What would you put into the empty bucket first—the big rocks, the pebbles, or the sand?

If you're thinking clearly, you would put the big rocks in first. The bucket may look full, but there will be a many empty spaces between the big rocks. Now you can add the pebbles and let them fill in those empty spaces. Again, the bucket may look full, but there are empty spaces around the pebbles. Now the sand can be poured in and allowed to flow into the empty spaces.

Think of Quadrant 2 activities as the "big rocks" of your life. To get them done, you have to proactively put them into your schedule first and let the other activities fill in the empty spaces around them. Do this and you will be amazed at how much time you have.

Going back to our bucket illustration, what would happen if you put the sand or pebbles in first? Obviously, the bucket would be "full" of sand and pebbles; there would be no room for the big rocks. Unfortunately, that's how most people schedule their time. They bounce from one "urgent" activity to the next and rarely get around to what's truly important.

Increasing our Quadrant 2 activities can help us have fewer "urgent" things to deal with. For example, how much time do you waste looking for missing items? You're about to leave for work, but you can't find your briefcase, your papers, or your car keys. So you decide that developing an organizational system would be a good Quadrant 2 activity. Once you have invested the time, you will waste a lot less time looking for lost items. You will spend less time in the "urgent" Quadrants.

So in the end, increasing Quadrant 2 activities saves both time and stress.

Many of the activities necessary to complete your *Consider It Done!* Behavior Change Project are Quadrant 2 activities. As such, you will have to put them into your schedule in advance and let less important activities fill in the spaces around them. This takes practice, but it can make a world of difference.

Coach's Corner

In this Coach's Corner, we will look at Brad's calendar for the week. Imagine it's Sunday night, and Brad is beginning to review his plans for the week. He has already blocked off several important but non-urgent activities. Some involve work-related issues while others pertain to other areas of his life.

Monday	
09:00 Workout	14:00
10:00 Weekly goal setting	15:00 Phone session with coach
11:00 Strategic planning with staff	16:00
12:00 Prayer and devotional time	17:00
13:00	18:00
Tuesday	
09:00 Professional reading	14:00
10:00	15:00 Planning session with sales team
11:00	16:00
12:00 Prayer and devotional time	17:00
13:00	18:00

Wednesday	
09:00 Workout	14:00
10:00 Meet with Bill on new product ideas	15:00 Conference with son's teacher
11:00	16:00
12:00 Prayer and devotional time	17:00
13:00	18:00
Thursday	
09:00 Professional reading	14:00
10:00	15:00 Team-building session
11:00	16:00
12:00 Prayer and devotional time	17:00
13:00	18:00 Dinner out with Joan

Friday	
09:00 Workout	14:00
10:00	15:00 Weekly goal review
11:00 Reorganize filing system	16:00
12:00 Prayer and devotional time	17:00
13:00	18:00

Saturday	
09:00 Prayer and devotional time	14:00 Scout troop planning meeting
10:00	15:00
11:00	16:00 Nature hike with kids
12:00	17:00
13:00	18:00

Sunday	
09:00	14:00
10:00	15:00
11:00 Church service with family	16:00 Weekly planning with Joan
12:00	17:00
13:00 Weekly family meeting	18:00

4

Are you Ready to Change?

In their book *Changing for Good* (Avon Books, 1995), James Prochaska, John Norcross, and Carlo DiClemente outline the six stages of any significant behavioral change:

> **Pre-contemplation:** You are not even considering making a change. If your current behavior is causing problems, you are either unaware of the problems or the problems do not seem significant enough to warrant change.

> **Contemplation:** You are considering a behavior change. You see the benefit of changing, and you begin to imagine what it would be like if your behavior were different.

Preparation: You are seriously considering a change and are taking preliminary steps to prepare yourself to change. You plan to change within the next 30 days.

Action: You have committed to change and are taking concrete steps to change your behavior.

Maintenance: You have had some success in changing your behavior. However, you still need to take steps to maintain these changes, and you must be vigilant not to revert back to your old habits.

Termination: Your new behaviors are so well established that you're never tempted to return to your old habits. There is very little chance you will relapse.

Knowing which stage you are in will help you understand what you need to do to move ahead. We will use the case of Stacey to illustrate these stages.

Stacey's Story

Stacey is a 36-year-old marketing consultant who has smoked cigarettes since she was 15.

Pre-contemplation

From the ages of 15 to 32, Stacey was in the *Pre-contemplation* stage. During this time, she didn't see her smoking as a problem, and she had no intention of stopping. Occasionally her mother would warn her of the dangers of smoking, but she wouldn't pay much attention.

Sadly, many people with problem behaviors remain in the *Pre-contemplation* stage all their lives. It usually takes a consciousness-raising experience to move a person from one stage to the next.

Contemplation

When she was 32, Stacey began to notice that many of her friends were kicking the habit. She used to love joining her co-workers in the staff lounge for cigarette breaks. Then smoking was banned in her office building, and Stacey was forced to take her breaks outside. One day she accidentally burned a hole in her favorite sweater with a cigarette.

For the first time ever, Stacey entered the *Contemplation* stage, that is, she started thinking about quitting. She used to avoid reading material on the dangers of smoking, now she sought out that same information. She started to consider making a change, but she didn't take any concrete action.

Preparation

Stacey thought about quitting for about 18 months. She even made a few half-hearted attempts to cut down, but with little commitment behind her efforts, she didn't succeed.

Then she learned that her favorite uncle was dying of lung cancer. Uncle Steve had smoked for as long as Stacey could remember, and now he was gravely ill. That was all Stacey needed to move into the *Preparation* stage. A person in this stage has a higher motivation level and a clear intention of changing behavior within 30 days.

During this time, Stacey started telling people that she was going to quit. She had never done this before because she was afraid of being embarrassed if she failed. Now she didn't care. She started reading about programs to help her stop smoking. She read about the nicotine patch and decided to make an appointment with her doctor as soon as she finished an important project at work.

She had not quit yet, but she was gearing up for it.

Action

Next came the big day when Stacey entered the *Action* stage. She put on the patch and threw her remaining cigarettes away. She used lollypops and carrot sticks to satisfy her oral cravings. She consulted a psychologist who taught her behavioral management techniques. When she felt a craving to smoke, she practiced relaxation techniques to reduce stress. At times she was miserable, but she was also excited at the prospect of becoming a non-smoker. For the first time, she started to believe that she could quit smoking forever.

A Step Backward

Stacey maintained a consistent focus and remained smoke-free for more than three months. Then complacency set in. From time to time, she would be out with friends and would bum a cigarette just for "old time's sake." Then she was given a promotion at work that required very long hours and subjected her to enormous stress. That was all it took; within two weeks, she was back to smoking a pack and a half a day.

Even though she was quite frustrated and even disgusted with herself, Stacey did not go all the way back to the *Pre-contemplation* stage. She had learned too much to ever be totally resigned to smoking again. So she slipped back into the *Contemplation* stage. She smoked every day, but now she knew she could quit if she was consistent in her effort.

After six months on the new job, Stacey was more relaxed and felt ready to try again. She prepared herself to take action. This time, however, she did not relapse. She learned from her past mistakes and stayed with her program until she was completely tobacco-free for six months.

Stacey was delighted with herself. Her clothes no longer reeked of cigarette smoke, and she was no longer exiled to the lonely smoking section outside her office.

Maintenance

Buoyed by her success, Stacey entered the *Maintenance* stage. As the name implies, this stage involves maintaining the changes that were made during the *Action* stage. Stacey must still be careful to avoid situations that might trigger a relapse. However, being a non-smoker feels more natural to her now, so she doesn't have to work as hard at it.

Termination

Stacey remained in the *Maintenance* stage for more than two years before she was finally able to enter the *Termination* stage. In this stage, she no longer felt any desire to smoke. In fact, the very idea of smoking was now repugnant to her so there was very little chance that she would ever resume it.

For some destructive habits, the *Termination* stage never occurs, and *Maintenance* must be a life-long process. For example, most recovering alcoholics will tell you that they expect to be in the *Maintenance* stage for the rest of their lives.

Progress at Any Stage

As a clinician and Coach, I can help my clients make progress no matter what stage they are in. To illustrate, I once had a clinical client with a severe long-standing alcohol and marijuana dependence. Ken had been thinking about the impact of these substances, and he knew that it would be best if he quit (i.e., *Contemplation*). I advised him that when he was ready to quit, he would need more than just our therapy sessions. I recommended regular Narcotics Anonymous (NA) and Alcoholics Anonymous (AA) meetings.

During one of our sessions, Ken made a commitment to go to NA or AA meetings, but when he returned for the following session, he had not done so. Rather than berate him, I told him that we had been premature. Instead of an *Action* step, he needed a *Preparation* step. During the following week, he agreed to write a list of the pros and cons of quitting and use that to help him decide whether to take the next step. The key was to keep him moving forward, not to push him into something he was not ready to do.

Can you identify the stage that you're in on your Behavior Change Project? Since you are considering taking this Project on, you must at least be in the *Contemplation* stage. But are you ready to take action to accomplish your goals? Be patient with yourself if you are not yet in the *Action* stage. If you are ready, great! Let's get going. However, if you aren't sure you're ready, read on anyway.

The next Chapter covers the First Prescription for any Behavior Change Project. After following this First Prescription, you'll know whether you have the desire to proceed further. It's about getting "fueled" for the task at hand.

5

Prescription 1: *Find the Payoffs*

You can't go anywhere without fuel. For any Behavior Change Project, your fuel is your motivation. What are your reasons for wanting to complete this project? What's in it for you? What's in it for the people you care about? Visualize these benefits as clearly as you can.

Then, write *specific, detailed descriptions of how you will benefit*. I call these your Payoffs. Write them in the first person, present tense as if you are already enjoying the Payoff. For example, "I've lost 30 pounds, and I'm wearing the beautiful blue dress to my high school reunion. People are staring at me and they're amazed at how good I look." Write as many of these as you can. The benefits can be modest ("My increased commissions have helped me buy new bedroom furniture"), or audacious and extravagant ("I have a beautiful 10,000 square foot home," or "I'm donating $1,000,000 to my favorite charity.")

I always urge my clients to make their descriptions as vivid and emotionally laden as possible. Rather than saying, "My health is better," say something like, "I see my daughter getting married. I am able to hold my grandchildren." You get the picture. If it's something you want, ham it up a little!

You may be tempted to dismiss this Prescription as a waste of time. "I know the reasons I'm doing this. I don't need to write them down." I understand your skepticism, but I urge you to do it anyway. The extra time will be well worth it.

There are two types of Payoffs. The first type is tangible and involves an external reward such as money, a job, or a material possession (e.g. "I love driving my new Lexus."). The second type is more internal and intangible (e.g., "My high school counselor told me that I'd never make it through college. I call him to tell him he was wrong.") It is often the internal and intangible payoffs that offer the greatest motivation.

✓ The more clearly you visualize your Payoffs, the more motivated you will be. Some people are more visual than others, but everyone can develop their powers of visualization with sustained practice. Here's how a Coach might help you develop a clearer vision.

Coach's Corner

Dave's Coach helps him to increase his motivation by figuring out what the Payoffs are for his work.

Coach: "Dave, you said one of the reasons you'd like to increase your sales commissions was that you want to buy a new home. Do you want to buy in an established neighborhood or build a new house?"

Dave: "We really like the Village Park community, so we thought we might look in there."

Coach: "Great. What is it about that area that appeals to you?"

Dave: "We've met some of the people, and it seems like a nice place to live. It's very convenient to my office, and we know that the schools are great."

Coach: "So I guess it would mean a lot to you to get your kids into that school district."

Dave: "Absolutely, we've checked this out pretty thoroughly, and we know that the schools are vastly superior to where we live now."

Coach: "I bet you can just picture enrolling your kids in those outstanding schools."

Dave: "Yes. It's a great image!"

Coach: "Sounds like something that could motivate you to make those extra sales calls."

Dave:	"I never thought about it that way, but I guess you're right."
Coach:	"You were also saying that this area is closer to your office."
Dave:	"Yes, it would save me about an hour of commuting time each day."
Coach:	"Sounds great. What would you do with the extra time?"
Dave:	"Have time with my kids. If I could get home earlier, we could all play outside until it gets dark. As it is now, I don't feel like I have enough time for them."
Coach:	"So when you feel reluctant to make that next sales call, would it be helpful to picture being able to play with your kids?"
Dave:	"Absolutely!"

Can you see how the Coach has helped Dave? From now on, Dave is not just trying to increase his commissions; he is placing his kids in those good schools and having more time to play with them. Do you see the difference?

Do you think that Dave will now be more likely to make those sales calls?

What will his attitude be like on the sales calls?

Now it's your turn. In the space provided, write your reasons for wanting to complete your Behavior Change Project—your Payoffs. Be sure to make your Payoffs vivid and specific, rich with detail. What are you experiencing when you attain your goal? Where are you? What are you feeling? Who else is there? What are they saying to you? Here are more examples to help you get started:

> *For quitting smoking:* "I enjoy excellent health. I can climb stairs without getting winded. I live long enough to enjoy my grandchildren. I have almost no risk of lung cancer, heart disease, or emphysema. I don't cough."

> *For completing a college degree:* "My parents come to the commencement ceremony and are very proud of me. My old friends are impressed. I get a high-paying job with a Fortune 500 corporation. I'm earning $100,000. I have a great sense of accomplishment because I finished something that once seemed impossible."

Table 5.1: My Payoffs - "When I complete my Behavior Change Project, I..."
1.
2.
3.
4.
5.

Are your Payoffs vivid and specific?

Before going on to the next Prescription, there is one more thing to do. Next to each Payoff, write a specific date by which you expect to be enjoying that Payoff. For example, if you plan to purchase a house within a year, mark the date as a year from today. It won't really be a goal unless you put a date on it. Until then, it is just a fantasy.

Many people resist putting a date on their dreams. They fear that they will feel like a failure if they don't achieve their goals by that date. Don't worry about that. It helps to have a date to shoot for even if you don't make it. You can always reset it.

CHAPTER

6

Prescription 2: Be Sure Your Payoffs Match Your Values

The First Prescription concerns finding out what your fuel is. This Prescription ensures that the fuel is of good quality. To do this, you must determine whether your Payoffs are consistent with your values and moral beliefs.

Begin by asking yourself questions like these: "Is it morally right to increase my income by 30 percent?" "Is trying to lose weight a worthwhile goal or just a vanity?" You may seek the opinion of a pastor, priest, rabbi, or a trusted friend. You are more likely to succeed with your Behavior Change Project if you have decided that it is the *right* thing to do.

Here are some other questions to ask: "Will this goal add value to my life and to the lives of other people?" "Is this goal consistent with my religious beliefs or moral code?" "Will reaching this goal harm anyone else?"

A word of caution: Sometimes what we think of as moral values are really the result of unhealthy attitudes that we may have developed early in life. For example, if your parents were not financially successful, and they held negative opinions of wealthy people, you have gotten the idea that it is "bad" to be wealthy. But is financial success that is achieved by ethical and honorable means really "bad?"

Likewise, if your parents said things like, "You'll never amount to anything," you may have the mistaken belief that you are not "supposed" to succeed at anything. However, as an adult, you can evaluate these underlying beliefs and decide for yourself if they are valid.

As you sort through your motives, you may find a combination of noble and not-so-noble motives. For example, "I want to lose weight because I want to be a good role model for my children" is a very noble motive.

However, "I want to lose weight because I want to make my old friends jealous," is not so noble. I believe that it's okay to have both noble and not-so-noble motives. We are all imperfect creatures and none of us can hope to be completely pure and honorable in all of our motives. However, selfish motives alone usually do not lead to long-term success. We are more likely to reach our goals if our goals are consistent with our moral values.

Coach's Corner

Teresa's Coach helps her realize her Payoffs are consistent with her moral values and that the guilt she feels for increasing her income is just her old Gremlin speaking.

Teresa: "This may sound crazy to you, but the thought of increasing my income makes me feel a little guilty."

Coach: "It's good that you're in touch with that. Otherwise, we might waste a lot of time spinning our wheels. What is it about the extra income that makes you feel guilty?"

Teresa: "I guess I just don't want to be greedy. I don't know if it's right to make that much money."

Coach: "It sounds like it's important for you to do the right thing. You won't be successful if you're not acting in accordance with your moral values. Let's break this down a little. To make the extra money, you have to make more sales. Is there anything morally wrong about the things you have to do to make the sales?"

Teresa: "Not at all. I believe it's a great product and it's a great value to my customers. Most are really happy with the product and we give them an absolute money-back guarantee. I feel really good about what I'm doing."

Coach:	"So there's nothing wrong about the way you get the money, right?"
Teresa:	"I guess not."
Coach:	"So if the way you get the money is moral, is there anything wrong with having the money?"
Teresa:	"Not really, it's just that no one in my family has ever achieved this level of success. It's difficult for me to get used to the idea that I could have so much more than they ever had."
Coach:	"So rather than being a moral issue, it's more an issue of your image of yourself as part of your family. Is that right?"
Teresa:	"Yeah, I'll have to get used to the idea of having so much money, but at least I know it's not a bad thing."

It is important to Teresa that her behavior be consistent with her moral values. I hope it is also important to you that you do the right thing. If so, take some time to sort out the motives behind your payoffs and decide if they are consistent with your values. Complete the table on the next page.

Table 6.1: Are My Payoffs Consistent with My Values?	
Payoff	*Consistent with My Values? (Y/N)*
1.	
2.	
3.	
4.	
5.	

7

Prescription 3: Constantly Remind Yourself of the Payoffs

Now that you know your Payoffs and are sure that they're aligned with your values, you will need to find ways to continuously remind yourself of them. The first two Prescriptions concerned finding and evaluating the fuel. The Third Prescription enables you to constantly refuel so you don't run out of gas!

This is a crucial step; you must keep your reasons in front of you. No matter how strong your motivation is at first, it will wane as time passes. The problem is that you will "forget" your reasons. When you start to sweat and feel sore, you'll "forget" why you wanted to exercise. When it's time for final exams, you'll forget why you wanted your college degree. The process will go faster and be a lot more fun if you never forget why you're doing it.

Here are some ways to keep your reasons in front of you:

1. Read your list of Payoffs (from the First Prescription) every day.

2. Record your Payoffs on audiotape and play the tape to yourself regularly.

3. Find pictures that represent your Payoffs. If you want to lose weight, find pictures of thin people. Post these pictures on your refrigerator,   bathroom mirror, or in any other location that you see every day.

4. Find other tangible items that remind you of your Payoffs (e.g., travel brochures, house plans, etc.)

I have been amazed at the creativity some clients show in their efforts to stay highly motivated. One of my favorites was the high school student who was struggling to improve his grades so he could graduate with his classmates. He frequently went into the school auditorium and walked across the stage where he would receive his diploma. He vividly imagined what that event would be like. Not surprisingly, he made it!

Coach's Corner

Susan is concerned that she will lose motivation for her weight-loss Project. Her Coach helps her find a way to keep her Payoffs in front of her.

Coach: "Susan, you have some powerful reasons for wanting to lose 20 pounds, don't you?"

Susan: "Yes, I do. When I read over the list of Payoffs, I find myself feeling both excited and scared."

Coach: "Tell me about the scared feeling first."

Susan: "Talking to you now, it's easy to remember why I want to lose the weight. My motivation is strong now. But I know myself all too well. When I get the urge to eat something I shouldn't, all I can think about is how much I want the food. The Payoffs will be wonderful, but I'll forget them at the first sign of temptation."

Coach: "So you're concern is that you'll 'forget' your Payoffs, right?"

Susan: "Right, I just won't think about them."

Coach: "So would it help if you had some powerful ways to keep reminding yourself of your Payoffs? Some way to keep them constantly in front of you?"

Susan: "I think that would help."

Coach:	"Good. Let's begin by looking at some of your more powerful Payoffs. Which one gets to you emotionally?"
Susan:	"Well, I guess my most emotional Payoff has to do with the way I look. If I could just be a size eight again, I would feel great about myself. I was looking in a catalog yesterday and there was an outfit that I would look great in, but only if I can be a size eight."
Coach:	"I have a radical idea. How about you go ahead and buy that outfit? Then, when it arrives, hang it up someplace where you would see it every day. Don't hide it away in your closet. Put it out where you couldn't miss it. It would be your daily reminder of what you're trying to do."
Susan:	"That outfit costs quite a bit. If I bought it now, I'd have to reach my goal or else waste a lot of money."
Coach:	"That's the idea!"

Right now, decide how you are going to keep your Payoffs in front of you. Will you read your list every day? If not every day, how often will you read it? What else are you willing to do to help sustain a high level of motivation? Write your plan in the table below.

Table 7.1: I'll Remind Myself of My Payoffs by...
1.
2.
3.
4.
5.

Review

Let's stop and review the first three Prescriptions. The First Prescription enables you to determine your Payoffs. The Second Prescription helps you figure out if the Payoffs are aligned with your values. The Third Prescription helps ensure that you're constantly aware of what your Payoffs are. These all concern the "why" of what you're trying to do. It's easy to get fired up when we focus on the Payoffs.

The next Prescription is aimed at helping us understand and accept the price we have to pay in order to get the Payoffs we desire.

Consider it Done!

8

Prescription 4: Accept the Price You'll have to Pay

It's at this point that one of your first Gremlins may rear its ugly head. I call it the "lack of acceptance" Gremlin. You experience this Gremlin as you confront the obvious but unpleasant reality that there will be a price to pay to achieve your Payoffs. Here's the price: You will have to do things that you don't want to do. You will have to give up things that you don't want to give up. And, you will experience unpleasant feelings that you would rather avoid.

You will make better progress when you have emotionally accepted this price and are willing to pay it. You may still not "want" to pay it, but you are "willing" to pay it.

Perhaps you have heard of the "stages of acceptance" first outlined by Elizabeth Kubler-Ross in 1969. The stages are *Denial, Anger, Bargaining, Depression,* and *Acceptance.* If you're not making progress, perhaps you're stuck in one of the earlier stages.

I'll use a weight-loss program to illustrate this process. Bill is 52 years old and 40 pounds overweight. He also has a serious cholesterol problem. He has been advised by his doctor and urged by his family to lose weight.

Bill's first reaction may be *Denial.* He may be unwilling or unable to see the problem. Even if he sees the problem, he will not consider taking any initiative to correct it. He may "wish" he could lose weight, but he will delude himself by thinking that the problem will just "get better" without his taking any direct action.

As time passes and his health gets worse, Bill may proceed into the *Anger* stage. His attitude may be, "It's not fair; other people can eat what they want and still be thin. Why can't I? If they had my (job/wife/family/money problems), they'd be overweight too." A person stuck in this stage is taking comfort in blaming others for his problems. He will not make any progress toward achieving his goals until he works through this stage.

The next stage may be *Bargaining.* In this stage, Bill may make an initial decision to change his behavior, but he seriously underestimates how difficult it will be. He may try to "cut down on fats" or "watch my calories," but he will not be prepared to pay much of a price. He may follow some aspects of his weight-loss program, but refuse to do others. As soon as the going gets tough, he is likely to quit.

Once his initial efforts to control his weight have failed, Bill may proceed to the *Depression* stage. Discouragement and an overwhelming sense of hopelessness may emerge. He will be convinced that he just doesn't have what it takes to lose weight. He will be very tempted to give up.

If Bill is to ever make any real progress, he must eventually proceed on to the *Acceptance* stage. The attitude that characterizes this stage is "I may not like it that I have to make these changes in my life, but I'm willing to do whatever it takes to achieve my goals." When he gets to the *Acceptance* stage, Bill experiences a sense of peace. He no longer wastes time and energy on the internal struggle. He doesn't get angry or blame others for his situation. He doesn't get down on himself. He just proactively does what needs to be done.

This Prescription takes a high level of self-awareness and honesty. I often ask my clients what stage they are in. Usually, they can give me a pretty honest and accurate answer. Just being aware of where they are helps them make a conscious decision to move on to the *Acceptance* stage. So what emotional stage are you in: *Denial, Anger, Bargaining, Depression,* or *Acceptance*? In the space below, write where you think you are and why.

Table 8.1: My Emotional Stage

Coach's Corner

Susan continues to work toward her weight-loss goal. Her Coach helps her realize that she is under attack from the "lack of acceptance" Gremlin. She will make more progress when she becomes willing to pay the price.

Susan: "Okay, I'm ready to start losing weight."

Coach: "Great, have you written down some of the things you need to do?"

Susan: "Yes, here's my list."

Coach: "What's the first thing?"

Susan: "I need to drink at least 48 ounces of water a day. That's at least six eight-ounce glasses. Wow, I see a problem right off the bat. I spend most of my day at the office, and the water in our office fountains is not fit to drink. I would have to bring in filtered water from home."

Coach: "So how about bringing some water from home?"

Susan: "But you see, I already have to take in my laptop and planner every morning. I would have to make an extra trip back to my car to get the water."

Coach: "Are you willing to make the extra trip?"

Susan: "No way, it's a very long walk, and I have to go up a lot of steps. And what if the weather is bad?"

Coach: "So you're not willing to make the extra trip?"

Susan: "I guess not."

Coach: "Okay. Would you like to put our heads together and see if there's another way for you to get the water you need?"

Susan: "There isn't another way."

Coach: "So where are we?"

Susan: "Stuck, I guess."

Coach: "I guess you're right. With your permission, let's look at the facts. The very first step in your weight loss plan is to drink 48 ounces of water per day. The only way to do this is to make an extra trip back to the car for the water. But you are not willing to do that. What does it say to you that you're not willing to make the extra trip to accomplish your goals?"

Susan: "It sounds like I'm not motivated, doesn't it?"

Coach: "Tell me how come it sounds that way to you."

Susan: "Like you said, I say that I want to lose weight, but I'm not willing to do this one little thing to make it happen. I guess I was hoping that it would be easier. Maybe I should rethink this whole thing."

Coach: "There's no law that says you have to lose weight. If you're not willing to do the work then don't do it."

Susan:	"But I do want to lose weight, I think."
Coach:	"Remember when we talked about the stages that we go through on the way to Acceptance? What stage would you say you're in?"
Susan:	"I don't sound like I'm in Acceptance, do I? Maybe I'm in Bargaining, or maybe Anger. I realize that I keep arguing with the suggestions you give me. Maybe my motivation just isn't strong enough to get me to do the work."
Coach:	"Why don't we go back and review your original reasons for wanting to lose weight in the first place. Let's see if the Payoffs are really important enough for you to do the work."
Susan:	"Sounds good to me."

In this example, Susan said that she wanted to lose weight, but was bargaining with the process. It's as if she were saying, "Yes, I want to lose weight, but I want it to just magically happen. I don't want to have to do anything to make it happen." Susan will make no progress until she accepts what she has to do.

If you're stuck on this stage, here are your options:

1. Give up on this idea and wait until you're really ready to make the change.

2. Go back to the First Prescription and review your reasons for wanting to do this.

3. Read on to the Fifth Prescription. Perhaps finding an "Accountability Partner" will give you just the spark you need to keep going.

9

Prescription 5:
Find an
Accountability Partner

One reason we fail to reach our goals is that we approach them with a "Lone Ranger" mentality. We think that we must organize and carry out the project on our own without help from anyone else. Too often, this attitude leads to frustration and failure.

You need someone to encourage you, support you, and hold you accountable. Most of us have no problem with the "encourage" and "support" parts, but many of us recoil at the thought of being held accountable.

We don't like being held accountable, because for much of our lives accountability has been foisted upon us. We had no choice. We have been accountable to parents, teachers, and bosses whether or not we wanted to be.

This kind of accountability is different in three ways. First, it's about being accountable to yourself for a goal you've committed to reaching. Second, you choose the individual—your Accountability Partner—who will support and encourage you...and remind you of your commitment. Third, this accountability is thoroughly voluntary. No one is making you be accountable. You are choosing to be accountable.

Who should serve as your Accountability Partner? He or she must be encouraging and supportive and yet willing to gently confront you if you don't do what you say you're going to do. You need to feel as if you can be completely honest with him/her.

You and your Accountability Partner may choose to be accountable to each other. My Accountability Partner in writing this book was my close friend, Dr. Wayne Parker. Wayne was also writing a book. We gave each other regular e-mail progress reports. We even had a little friendly competition. I would never have finished this book without knowing I was accountable to him.

As a professional Coach, I often serve as the Accountability Partner for my clients. My clients know that I will ask them what they have done. Many have told me that was the key to finishing their Projects. I believe that accountability is one of the most powerful aspects of the coaching process.

Even though a professional Coach is probably the best Accountability Partner, a trusted friend, relative, or colleague will also do.

Your spouse can also be an Accountability Partner, but I would caution you to be very careful about selecting your spouse for this role. There is a level of emotional connection between spouses that makes it all but impossible to be objective and detached. It won't do if your Accountability Partner gets angry and frustrated with you or if his/her feedback hurts your feelings. Therefore, unless your marriage is incredibly strong, I would suggest you choose someone other than your spouse.

Right now, find someone to be your Accountability Partner. To explain to the person what the role entails, you might say something like, "Steve, I would like your help in keeping me on track as I write my dissertation. Would it be all right if I sent you a list of my goals each week? At the end of the week, I'll tell you what I actually accomplished. If I don't meet my goals for the week, I'll need you to gently push me. I think it will take me about three months to finish. Would you be able to help?"

Accountability sessions can be in person, by phone, or e-mail. It's important to end each session with specific action steps to be completed by some designated date (e.g., "I will finish Chapter 1 by September 15.")

Asking someone to serve as your Accountability Partner and then being answerable to this person may take some courage and humility, but it might well be the secret to your success.

Coach's Corner

Thomas needs to be more proactive in marketing his business. He decides to be accountable to his Coach.

Coach: "So you've decided to make at least five new business contacts this week. To whom do you want to be accountable?"

Thomas: "How about you?"

Coach: "That's fine. How will I know if you've made the contacts?"

Thomas: "How about if I keep a running log of all my contacts? After three days, I'll send you an e-mail telling you how I've done up to that point. Then I'll give you a full report when we talk next week."

Coach: "Sounds like a great plan. How do you want me to handle it if you haven't reached your goal?"

Thomas: "I'm pretty sure I can make it. But just in case I don't, I would expect you to push me a little bit and not let me get away with any excuses."

Coach: "That's fine with me."

In this case, the Coach agreed to be the Accountability Partner, but you can choose anyone you want.

Good luck finding your Accountability Partner!

10

Prescription 6: Inoculate Yourself Against "Excusitis"

In his wonderful book, *The Magic of Thinking Big* (Prentice Hall, initially published in 1959), Dr. David Schwartz coined the term "excusitis" which he defined as "the failure disease." No matter how motivated you are at first, Dr. Schwartz explained, you will eventually be tempted to procrastinate or quit. At this moment, your mind (i.e., your "Excuse Gremlin") will start to generate excuses. You'll have thoughts such as, "This is too hard" or "I don't feel like it today; I'll do it tomorrow" or "I don't have enough time to do it all today, so there's no sense in starting." Before you know it, excusitis takes over and kills your motivation and enthusiasm for your Behavior Change Project.

Whenever you get stuck on something important, I guarantee that your "Excuse Gremlin" is speaking. The secret is to stop and pay attention to your self-talk.

My clients and I have had a lot of fun with this concept. I tell them that it reminds me of the Donald Duck comic books that I read as a kid. Donald was an irritable and impulsive sort who often acted in ways that he regretted later.

When Donald was stuck in a moral dilemma, we would see two miniature Donald Ducks perched on his shoulder. On his right shoulder would be an angel and on his left, a devil. The devil was Donald's Gremlin who gave him the excuses he needed not to do what he was supposed to do. We all have that little devil, don't we?

The best way to deal with excusitis is to inoculate yourself against it. To do this, you must first make a list of all of the excuses that you are likely to use.

It may take time to identify your favorite excuses. Your Coach or Accountability Partner can help with this process. See if you can come up with 10 of your favorite excuses. Here are a few popular ones: "I don't have time," "I just don't feel like it," and "I'm too tired to today." Record yours in the space below.

Table 10.1: My Excuses
When I start feeling like I'm going to quit, what am I telling myself that's keeping me from taking the next step?
1.
2.
3.
4.
5.
6.
7.
8.
9.
10.

Now that you have all of your excuses down on paper, "inoculate" yourself against each one. To do this, write a gentle but firm rebuttal for each excuse. The rebuttal shouldn't be harsh or condemning (e.g., "You're just making excuses. Get off your butt, you lazy jerk"). Those kinds of rebuttals tend to demoralize you. Instead, your rebuttal should acknowledge that there is some truth to the excuse (e.g., " Yes, I am tired. Nevertheless…"), and then correct what may be inaccurate or irrational in the excuse.

Here is a basic example. We might have an excuse like, "I've worked so hard. I'm so tired. I just don't feel like working on my Project right now." A good rebuttal would be, "Yes, I have worked hard and I am tired. Nevertheless, I can do a little more work. Then I can rest and really feel good about myself."

Notice that the key word is "nevertheless." Yes, there are always good excuses for quitting. Nevertheless, you can take the next step.

If you have a Coach, ask him/her to help you write a gentle rebuttal to each excuse. If you don't have a Coach, ask your Accountability Partner to help you. Write your rebuttals down on index cards and review them regularly. Commit some of them to memory. Whenever you find yourself bogged down on your Project, identify your excuses and review your rebuttals.

I have found that once I have committed a few rebuttals to memory, I'm immune to most of my excuses. My rebuttals are an automatic buffer against the clever strategies of the Excuse Gremlin.

Table 10.2: My Rebuttals	
When I start feeling like I'm going to quit, what am I telling myself that's keeping me from taking the next step?	*Instead of telling myself these things, I'll say, "Nevertheless..."*
1.	
2.	
3.	
4.	
5.	
6.	
7.	
8.	
9.	
10.	

Coach's Corner

Instead of my usual Coach's dialog, I have written some common excuses and sample rebuttals.

Excuse: "I don't have the time."

Rebuttal: "Maybe I only have a few minutes right now. Nevertheless, I can at least get started and get a few things finished."

Excuse: "I just don't feel like doing it now."

Rebuttal: "Maybe I don't feel like doing it. Nevertheless, I'll feel great once I get started and get something accomplished."

Excuse: "I'm too tired. I don't have the energy."

Rebuttal: "If someone gave me a million dollars to do this, I'd jump in with great enthusiasm. Energy is largely a matter of attitude. If I change my attitude, I'll have all the energy I need."

Excuse: "It's too hard."

Rebuttal: "Yes, it takes considerable effort. Nevertheless, if I keep at it, I can accomplish my goals."

Good luck writing your own excuses and rebuttals. The best way to achieve what you want is to have the courage to deny yourself any excuses!

11

Prescription 7: Break the Project into Small Steps

Imagine this scene: A delivery person comes to your door and announces that a food shipment is being made to your house. The shipment consists of all of the food that you will consume for the rest of your life. You look outside and see workers unloading pounds of meat, bread, fruits, vegetables, snacks, drinks, and desserts. Your whole yard is piled high with more food than you have ever seen. Undoubtedly, you would feel overwhelmed and say, "There's no way I'm ever going to eat all of that food." But that's exactly what you will do, little by little, day by day.

The process of breaking big projects down into small steps is a time-honored method of helping people finish what they start. It helps children complete their homework. If you give a fifth grader 30 long division problems, he feels overwhelmed and may not even get started. However, if you give him three problems and praise him for completing them, you'll be amazed at how much he gets done.

One of my smartest college professors gave us a five-page reading assignment every night. The key was that we could be given a pop quiz any day on these reading assignments. Knowing that we were accountable, most of us read our assignment every night. By the end of the semester, we had completed three books. If that professor had stood up at the beginning of the semester and said, "Your assignment this semester is to read these three textbooks," most of us would have been overwhelmed and probably wouldn't have done it.

If your Project seems too big, try breaking it down into its smallest parts. Suppose you want to make a job change, but you're too busy to spend a lot of time on the process. Perhaps you can do a little bit at a time. Your first step might be to update your resume. Then you might want to contact a "headhunter" or start searching the Internet or Help Wanted ads for job openings. String a few of these action steps together, and you'll get your new job.

Map your course step by step. When you get bogged down, just take the next step. Don't worry about getting everything done at once.

It's important that you put each step in writing. There are three ways to do this. The simplest is to just list the various tasks in order, being sure to attach a completion date to each task. You might create a table for yourself that looks something like this:

Table 11.1: Project Task List	
Step	*Completion Date*

If you're more the artistic type, you might want to produce a storyboard. A storyboard is used in the production of TV shows and movies. Each scene of the show is briefly described on cards and placed in their proper sequence so the flow of the plot can be visualized. Here is what a storyboard for a weight-loss program might look like:

Scene 1: Create list of payoffs for losing weight and start to review daily. **January 15**	**Scene 2:** Attend first Weight Watchers® meeting. **January 17**
Scene 3: Start keeping journal of everything I eat. **January 18**	**Scene 4:** Start drinking 6 glasses of water per day. **January 18**
Scene 5: Start walking one-mile three times a week. **January 25**	**Scene 6:** Start changing shopping habits to buy only healthy low-fat foods. **January 25**

Scene 7: Start eating within prescribed point/calorie level. **January 31**	**Scene 8:** Reach first goal of 10% weight loss. **March 31**

If a storyboard doesn't appeal to you, you might want to create a flowchart. Management and technical types will like these. A flowchart is much like a storyboard except that each "scene" is a box with a "Yes" or "No" option. Both the "Yes" and the "No" options lead to an action step. For example, a graduate student is working on his dissertation. One of the boxes on his storyboard reads "Proposal accepted by Committee." Flowing from the "No" option is a box that reads "Revise proposal." Flowing from the "Yes" box is another that reads "Start collecting data."

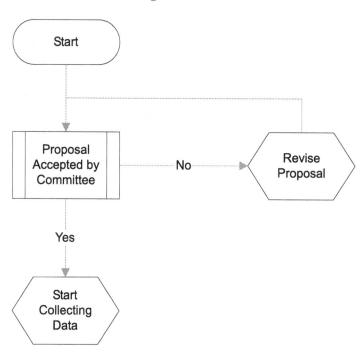

The feature I like most about flowcharts is the fact that even negative events (e.g., not having a proposal approved) lead to a specific, positive action rather than to despair or discouragement.

If you have a big dream or an audacious project ahead of you, it might help to spend some time breaking it down into smaller intermediate goals. Let your Coach or Accountability Partner help you with this. Of course, you may change your intermediate goals as you go along, but you need to start somewhere.

Visualize as best you can the sequence of steps you will have to take. Imagine yourself having completed one step and then imagine what the next step will be. If you find this process difficult, you may try imagining the process backwards. For example, what is the last step you will need to make? Then what is the step you will need to make just prior to that one? And so on.

In the table on the next page, write all the steps and intermediate goals that will eventually lead to achieving your larger goal and fulfilling your dream. (Continue on a separate sheet if necessary.) Be sure to attach a completion date to each of your intermediate goals. Don't worry if you can't reach each intermediate goal by its assigned date. You will still be better off for having the goal than having no goal at all. Please take the time to follow this Prescription. It will save you time in the long run.

Table 11.2: Project Intermediate Goals	
Project Name:	
Intermediate Goal	*Completion Date*
1.	
2.	
3.	
4.	
5.	
6.	
7.	
8.	
9.	
10.	

Consider it Done!

12

Prescription 8: Reward Yourself for the Completion of Each Step

This Prescription is the most fun to take. Having broken your big Behavior Change Project down into its smallest parts, you can start taking action. Just be sure to reward yourself when you complete any of these small steps.

The reward doesn't have to be big. Maybe you can treat yourself to dinner at your favorite restaurant. Maybe you can rent that movie that you have wanted to see. The important thing is that it is something that you genuinely enjoy, and *you must be willing to deny yourself this reward until after the intermediate goal is completed.*

If you're a "self starter," you may be tempted to skip this step, thinking that you don't need it. However, we all need rewards. It's a basic principle of human behavior that applies to everyone, even you.

Coach's Corner

As Susan makes progress on her weight-loss goal, her Coach helps her find ways to reward herself.

Coach: "So it looks to me like you've developed an excellent plan to lose those 20 pounds. You have a storyboard for your various activities. You have a healthy diet and exercise plan, and you have an Accountability Partner. As you make progress on this, how are you going to reward yourself?"

Susan: "I've got that all figured out. When I lose five pounds, I'm treating myself to the latest Mel Gibson movie. Then at 10 pounds, I'm splurging on a full-hour massage at the health spa. At 15 pounds, I'm going on a shopping spree at the mall. And when I get to my ultimate goal of 20 pounds, my husband and I are going off for a long weekend in the mountains."

Coach: "I think you've got the hang of this. You didn't need me at all for that."

Now review the intermediate goals that you outlined in the previous Chapter. Write a reward that you will give yourself when you achieve each intermediate goal.

Table 12.1: Rewards for Achieving Intermediate Goals		
Project Name:		
Intermediate Goal	Completion Date	Reward
1.		
2.		
3.		
4.		
5.		
6.		
7.		
8.		
9.		
10.		

13

Prescription 9: Practice the Premack Principle

Use the "Desired" to reward the "Required"
- Dr. David Premack

T here is a concept in psychology called the Premack Principle first described by Dr. David Premack in the 1960s. Even though its power has been demonstrated by laboratory research, it's a principle that your grandmother understood very well. The principle is simple: "Popular" activities can be used as a reward for the completion of other activities.

Picture this: You're at home in the evening. You could do some work on your Project, but you just don't "feel" like doing it. You would much rather watch the baseball game on TV. Given these two choices, your emotional pull will be toward the baseball game. But if you watch the game, you will feel guilty afterward, and you won't have made any progress.

Around my house, we try to practice the Premack Principle. That is, we do what we have to first and then reward ourselves by doing at least a little of what we want to do. For example, I have watched the last inning of many a baseball game and thoroughly enjoyed it because I knew I had earned the right.

Coach's Corner

Brad uses the Premack Principle to balance family time, professional growth, and relaxation.

Brad: "To achieve the level of success I want, I will definitely have to do more professional reading. The problem is I have to do most of it at home in the evenings. But to tell you the truth, it's a lot more important to me to play with my kids. That's more fun and probably more important to me than doing the reading."

Coach: "Of course it's more fun and more important. Is there anything you do that is also more fun but not as important?"

Brad: "Well, I do like to watch TV. I know it's probably a waste of time, but I find it so relaxing after a long day."

> **Coach:** "So could you use TV watching as a reward for doing the more important things?"
>
> **Brad:** "I guess. I could spend some quality time with the kids just before dinner. We could even go outside if the weather is good. Then after dinner, they have to do their homework. They don't need much help these days, so I guess I could do my reading during homework hour. Then I could have a little more time with them before they go to bed."
>
> **Coach:** "And what about the TV watching?"
>
> **Brad:** "Once I've done everything else, I can stretch out and take in just a little bit before I go to bed. The great thing will be that I can do it without feeling guilty. I'll know that I will have really earned it."

You may be telling yourself, "But I don't have the discipline to deny myself the reward in the first place. I'll go ahead and watch TV anyway!"

That's your Gremlin speaking. You may have not followed the Premack Principle in the past, but that doesn't mean you're doomed never to follow it in the future.

"Self-discipline" is nothing more than the sum total of all of the choices we make. You can make wiser choices now because you have followed the previous Prescriptions.

Here is how you are different than you were before you started reading this book:

1. You understand the power of self-talk and how to overcome the Gremlin (Chapter 2).

2. You have fueled yourself for your project by getting in touch with the Payoffs, and you are constantly reminding yourself of these Payoffs (Chapters 5-7).

3. You have emotionally accepted that there will be a price to pay for obtaining the Payoffs. You will have to do things you don't want to do and give up things you don't want to give up (Chapter 8).

4. You have an Accountability Partner (Chapter 9).

5. You know how to overcome "excusitis" (Chapter 10).

6. You have broken the project down into its smallest parts, attached a completion date to each part, and decided how you will reward yourself when each part is completed (Chapters 11 and 12).

If you are struggling with any of these points, reread the Chapter that covers it. Let your Coach and/or Accountability Partner know where you are struggling.

If you have had at least some success in following the Prescriptions up to this point, you have the self-discipline necessary to apply the Premack Principle.

In the space below, write down how you plan to use the Premack Principle to help you with your Behavior Change Project.

Table 13.1: I will use the Premack Principle to motivate myself by...

14

Prescription 10: Overcome Fear with Action

Sometimes we don't take on Projects because we are afraid. We're afraid that we will fail. We're afraid of what others will think of us if we don't reach our goal. We're afraid that we don't have what it takes to complete the Project. Sometimes we allow this fear to paralyze us.

Maybe even reading this book makes you anxious. Maybe you fear that you'll get all excited about changing, only to fall back into all of your old habits. (Do you see how persistent the Gremlin is?) Sometimes it just feels safer not to try anything new.

To get past this fear, you must realize that it's not "doing" the task that makes us afraid. It's "thinking" about it. Remember when you had to do oral book reports in middle school? If you're like a lot of people, you probably dreaded it for days. However, once you started, you stopped being anxious, and it was over quickly.

When I played high school football, I always dreaded game day. The closer it got to game time, the more afraid I was. But again, I wasn't playing the game at that point, I was thinking about playing. Once the game started, I was too busy to be afraid.

Here's a diagram that I often share with my clients. Notice that we have the Comfort Zone on the left. To get to Success, Achievement, and Growth, you have to leave your Comfort Zone and travel through Discomfort, Anxiety, and Fear.

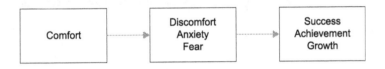

It's inevitable. Think of anything that you have accomplished in life. Didn't you have to go through some discomfort, anxiety, and/or fear to get there?

If you put off doing things because of fear, you only add to your fear in the long run. The very best antidote to fear is action. Do the thing you fear, and the fear will go away. You may not believe me, but talk to any successful person and he or she will tell you the same thing. Stop thinking about it and start doing it.

So if fear is holding you back, take the following steps:

1. Review the First Prescription, that is, remind yourself why you wanted to complete this Project in the first place.

2. Make a commitment to your Accountability Partner that you are going to take action.

3. Take action.

If you're ready to take action, skip the next section. If you still need some help overcoming fear, read the next section carefully.

Fear Reduction Techniques

Let me teach you two simple techniques that can significantly reduce your fear and anxiety. One technique deals with the physical sensations of fear, the other with the thoughts that accompany fear. Both techniques are routinely used in the treatment of severe anxiety problems such as Panic Disorder, Specific Phobia, and Social Anxiety Disorder.

Deep Abdominal Breathing

Most people don't know this, but God has provided us with a natural tranquilizer that we can use any time. It is perfectly safe and has no side effects. It's called deep abdominal breathing. You may think you know how to breathe, but in reality most of us have "forgotten" how.

Watch a newborn baby breathe. Every time the baby inhales, its stomach will rise and then fall each time he exhales. Take that same child six years later, and ask him to "take a deep breath," you'll see something quite different. As the child inhales, his shoulders and chest will rise, but he will actually pull his stomach in, just the opposite of the newborn baby!

Millions of people have learned how relaxing and soothing it can be to return to the type of breathing we did as babies. It has been taught by everyone from yoga and meditation masters to behavioral psychologists. Take the time to master this technique, and you can instantly calm yourself no matter how stressful the situation.

Here's how to do it. Lie flat on your back. Place your right hand on your stomach and your left hand on your chest. As you slowly breathe in, your right hand should rise while your left hand remains stationary. Breathe in to a slow count of three and then breathe out to a slow count of three. As you exhale, your right hand should slowly descend. Repeat this process for three to five minutes. You may get a little dizzy. If you do, don't worry, just slow down the process for a few minutes.

This skill may be harder to master than it sounds, but keep practicing and eventually you'll get it. Of course, consult your physician if you have any condition that might make it difficult to apply this skill.

I use this technique all the time—in a room full of strangers, preparing to speak to a professional organization, or dealing with a conflict with someone I care about. I can instantly reduce my anxiety and create a greater sense of calm by taking just a few deep abdominal breaths. You can too!

Cognitive Restructuring

This technical-sounding term means simply that we change the way we think. Psychologists who study severe anxiety problems have discovered that our fears invariably stem from two common mental errors. To put it another way, our Gremlin lies to us in two different ways. Once we learn how to identify and modify these mental errors, we greatly reduce anxiety and worry.

Here's the first common mental error: We greatly overestimate the likelihood that some bad thing will happen. In other words, we believe something bad will happen that probably won't happen. For example, a job seeker may delay calling for an interview because he is convinced that he will make a complete fool of himself. However, when he looks objectively at his situation, he can see that he has been through interviews before, and though not all of them have gone smoothly, he has never made a fool of himself. Therefore, he isn't likely to do so now.

Of course, you might say that sometimes the bad thing <u>does</u> happen. That leads to the second common mental error. Even if the bad thing happens, we often overestimate how bad the consequences will be. For example, Susan has decided that she wants to lose weight. Since she has found it difficult to succeed on her own in the past, she feels she would do better if she joined a support organization such as Weight Watchers®. However, she is reluctant to attend the meetings, partly out of fear. She fears feeling awkward at the meeting and she fears being embarrassed by seeing someone she knows at the meeting. Yes, she might feel awkward and uncomfortable, especially at first. And yes, she might see someone she knows at the meeting. But so what? What would be the real consequence of either or both of these things happening?

Chances are that she would cope with either situation.

This technique sounds too simple, doesn't it? Nevertheless, I have seen countless victims of severe anxiety liberate themselves by following this simple model. If you're willing to change your thinking, you can also be freed from any fear that is holding you back. Talk to your Coach or Accountability Partner about this.

Coach's Corner

Leslie's Coach helps her face her fear of job interviews.

Coach: "Your long-term goal was to have a more fulfilling and higher-paying job by the end of the year. You've made great progress on your preliminary steps. You've submitted your resume to several of the top firms and several have responded. I guess it's time to go for those interviews."

Leslie: "Actually, I have been contacted by several companies, but I haven't scheduled any interviews yet."

Coach: "Is there anything getting in the way of scheduling the interviews?"

Leslie: "I have a lot of excuses, but the real reason is that I'm scared to death of interviews."

Coach: "Thank you for getting to the real reason and not wasting our time dealing with the excuses! What is it about interviews that you find so scary?"

Leslie: "I interviewed for my current position three years ago. I hardly got any sleep the week before the interview. This may sound crazy, but I had this thought that I would open my mouth but nothing would come out. I was so scared that I thought I would throw up. I even imagined throwing up during the interview!"

Coach: "So as the time for the interview got closer, you started imagining all of the bad things that might happen, right? Tell me, how did the interview itself go? Did you throw up?"

Leslie: "No, that would have been terrible."

Coach: "But it didn't happen. Did you open your mouth and nothing came out?"

Leslie: "No, it wasn't a great interview, but I was able to talk. In fact, the interviewer did a great job trying to help me relax."

Coach: "So you didn't throw up, and you were able to speak. That's good. How did the interview go?"

Leslie: "Well, I didn't get the job, if that's what you mean. It turns out they were looking for someone with different qualifications. I didn't feel too badly about it."

Coach: "How did you feel during the interview?"

Leslie: "Well, I was very nervous at first, but after a while I settled down and just answered the questions the best I could. The truth was that I wasn't as prepared as I needed to be. I would have been more relaxed if I had prepared more."

Coach: "You didn't have a Coach or anyone to practice with then, did you?"

Leslie: "No, but now I do!"

Coach: "So what have we learned from our work together that would help you get these interviews done?"

Leslie:	"Well, I know that the longer I put them off, the more I'll think about it, so I need to commit to a specific time. Then I have to prepare and practice with a buddy. Then I really need to think about what I'm really scared of and remind myself that I can handle it if I don't get the job. Then I need to practice my breathing. If I do all of that I should be okay."
Coach:	"Fantastic, you've learned a lot!"

Another final point about fear: It's uncomfortable, but it won't kill you, and it doesn't have to keep you from achieving your dreams. Just keep moving and you'll find that you can push through the fear and finish what you start.

Let's review the Ten Prescriptions:

1. Find Your Payoffs.

2. Be Sure Your Payoffs Match Your Values.

3. Constantly Remind Yourself of Your Payoffs.

4. Accept the Price You'll Have to Pay.

5. Find an Accountability Partner.

6. Inoculate Yourself Against "Excusitis."

7. Break the Project into Small Steps.

8. Reward Yourself for the Completion of Each Step.

9. Practice the Premack Principle: Use the Desired to Reward the Required.

10. Overcome Fear with Action.

Now you have the tools. Keep at it, and you'll be able to finish what you start!

15

Persistance: The Secret to Overcoming Discouragement

Y ou now have all the Prescriptions necessary to finish your Behavior Change Project. Have you already started? If not, will you start soon? Whenever you start, I hope you begin with great excitement and energy for the task at hand. After all, you have all those wonderful Payoffs in your future!

Maybe your Project will be a snap. Now that you're properly motivated, you might well just breeze through it in record time. That could happen! There is no law that says that it has to be difficult or tedious. If it's easy for you, count your blessings and enjoy your success.

On the other hand, you may get discouraged somewhere along the line and want to give up. The work may be harder than you expected. You may be way behind on your timetable. Those wonderful Payoffs may seem light-years away.

You've hit a dry spell. We've all seen those Western movies in which the hero is crossing the desert. The water is gone and his throat is parched. The vultures are circling overhead, preparing to pick at his carcass. This is how it can feel sometimes when you're bogged down on a Project and there appears to be no end in sight.

Other people may have expressed doubt in your ability to finish. You're starting to think that they're right. Maybe you just weren't meant to finish. Maybe you don't have the ability. Maybe you don't have the discipline and persistence to see this thing through to the end.

Your Gremlin is having a field day!

If you're feeling this way, I want to encourage you to quit! That's right, I want you to quit. I want you to quit *beating yourself up*. Remember that all that self-doubt and discouragement is just your Gremlin speaking. There may be an ounce of truth to what the Gremlin says, but you can be sure that there is a pound of lies. Use what you've learned to refute the Gremlin and move on.

In the space on the next page, write some of the negative things your Gremlin is saying to you now.

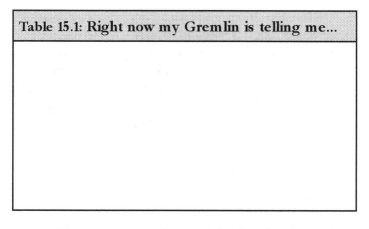

Table 15.1: Right now my Gremlin is telling me...

Here's an exercise that can help. Imagine that you're speaking to your best friend in the world. You have enormous respect and admiration for this person. Your friend has flaws, but you are able to see past those flaws to the quality person within. Your friend is discouraged because he/she is trying to accomplish a long-term goal but is stuck in the process.

You want to speak to your friend in the most encouraging way possible. You would probably want to acknowledge his/her discouragement. You would want to balance support and understanding with a little gentle pushing. You're likely to point out his/her successes in the past. You might remind him/her of the helpful resources that are available.

Imagine specifically what you would say to your friend and write it down in the space below.

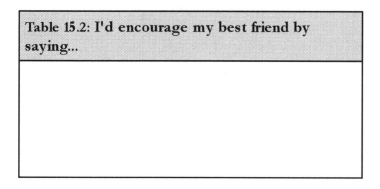

Table 15.2: I'd encourage my best friend by saying...

You can already guess what I'm going to suggest now. I want you to say these things to yourself. Maybe you don't have the same level of admiration and respect for yourself that you have for that best friend. That is okay. Just pretend that you have that level of self-respect and write your encouraging statements *as if* you did. This exercise can have a profoundly encouraging effect if you give it a chance.

Get "Locked In"

If you're like most people, your rate of progress may not be consistent. There may be periods of time when you seem to be going nowhere. Even the thought of working on your Project creates an unbearable sense of dread.

It just seems so big and overwhelming, so why bother? Those periods are agonizing indeed. These are the times when you just need to chip away and keep making use of the Ten Prescriptions.

Then there will be times when you're incredibly focused and productive. You will have a high level of energy, and you will make great progress in very short periods of time. Athletes talk about being "in the zone." I like the term "locked in." These are magical times, and you need to take advantage of them when they happen. You may find that much of your Project gets completed during these bursts of productivity.

Some Projects are well suited for the peaks and valleys of productivity. Writing a book or dissertation is such a project. There were times when I couldn't bear to even think about this book. During the bursts, however, I could barely type fast enough to get my thoughts down.

Other Projects require a more consistent and steady effort. For example, a weight-loss or exercise program will work best if you can give it your consistent attention on a daily basis.

Obviously, the more often we are "locked in," the faster our progress will be. When I'm struggling, I find it helpful to sit quietly and remember a recent time when I was locked in. Where was I? What did I do just prior to being locked in? I try to remember the feeling. Most of all, I need to not quit and have faith that the locked-in feeling will return.

In the space below, write about a time when you were very productive and felt "locked in."

Table 15.3: I felt "locked in" when...

Two More Strategies

Here are two more hints for overcoming discouragement.
First, when you get discouraged, review each of the Ten
Prescriptions. Go back to your Payoff list (The First Prescription). Read it over and over. Do you still want those Payoffs?
Look for more ways to remind yourself of your Payoffs (The
Third Prescription). Remember that the first three Prescriptions concern the motivation that is fueling your efforts.
Maybe you just need to be refueled.

The other Prescriptions can also help overcome
discouragement. Do you need to go back and accept the price
necessary to complete your Project (The Fourth Prescription)?
Do you need greater accountability (The Fifth Prescription)?

Are excuses keeping you from taking action (The
Sixth Prescription)? Do you need to break the Project into
small parts and reward yourself for any progress you make
(The Seventh, Eighth, and Ninth Prescriptions)? Is fear
getting in your way (The Tenth Prescription)? Reviewing any
relevant Prescription can help you work through any discouragement you may feel.

My other hint for overcoming discouragement will
seem strange. I want you to <u>welcome</u> discouragement. You
read it right. I want you to welcome discouragement. Here's
why: Remember that when you feel discouragement, it's
because of the negative self-talk of your Gremlin. When does
the Gremlin speak? It speaks whenever you're trying to
accomplish something new. It speaks whenever you step out
of your Comfort Zone to make some significant change in
your life.

In other words, the fact that you're discouraged must
mean that you are trying something new. It means you're
stretching yourself. If you never tried anything new, you
would never feel discouraged.

In fact, I have found that the closer that I get to my goal, the louder the Gremlin speaks. What started out as a soft whisper becomes a loud yell when it looks like I might actually finish what I've started.

I have noticed this in my clients as well. Many a graduate student stalls at the point in their dissertation when they are actually the closest to reaching their degree. Many people who are trying to lose weight quit just when they are about to reach their goal.

So now when I'm discouraged, I ask myself, "What is my Gremlin trying to stop me from doing? Am I going to let him do it?" I have come to regard periods of discouragement as minor rest periods during which I collect myself for the next surge of action.

Perhaps you've heard the story of the time Winston Churchill was asked to speak to a group of school children. Since he was considered one of the greatest orators of the 20th century, everyone was expecting a stirring speech. This was the sum total of his speech: "Never give up! Never give up! Never, never, never give up!" Then he sat down. That's all he had to say. That's all that needed to be said.

16

Celebrate, Celebrate, Celebrate!

Congratulations! You did it! You have completed your Behavior Change Project, and I sincerely hope you are enjoying the results. Take time to savor your victory and be sure to thank your Accountability Partner.

Are you fully enjoying the Payoffs of your success? In the space below, write about the Payoffs that mean the most to you now. Are they the tangible ones or the intangible ones?

Table 16.1: The Payoffs that mean the most to me are...
1.
2.
3.
4.
5.

Was there any time when you thought about giving up? In the space below, write down what kept you from giving up and encouraged you to keep on.

Table 16.2: What kept me from giving up?

Moving Forward

Now that you have achieved your goal, there may be some things you will have to do in order to maintain your progress. For example, if you achieved a weight-loss goal, you cannot revert to your old lifestyle if you hope to keep the weight off. You will still need to exercise and limit your food intake.

Likewise, if your goal was to develop a new business to a certain level, you may need to continue many of the behaviors that got you to where you are. However, I would guess that many of these behaviors are "natural" to you now, so they will not take that much effort.

If your Project will require some continuing attention, write down the specific plans you have to maintain your results. If you need help with this, talk with your Coach or Accountability Partner.

I have two personal favors to ask. First, I would love to receive your feedback about this book. What was good and what needs to be improved in future editions? You can contact us by phone, mail, or e-mail. Visit **www.drhibbs.com** for our contact information.

My second request is even more important to me. If there is anything in this book that was valuable to you, please pass it on to someone you care about. There is so much in this world that discourages and disheartens people. I love the idea that these concepts might bless many people that I will never know.

Again, congratulations on your success!

Bibliography

Burns, David. *The Feeling Good Handbook.* New York: Penguin Books, 1989. ISBN-10: 0-452-26174-0.

Covey, Stephen R. *The Seven Habits of Highly Effective People.* New York: Simon & Schuster, 1989. ISBN-10: 0-671-70863-5.

Ditzler, Jinny S. *Your Best Year Yet.* New York: Warner Books, 1994. ISBN-10: 0-446-66784-6.

Prochaska, James O. et al. *Changing for Good.* New York: Avon Books, 1994. ISBN-10: 0-380-72572-X.

Schwartz, David. *The Magic of Thinking Big.* New York: Simon & Schuster, 1987. ISBN-10: 0-671-64678-0. Originally published by Prentice Hall, 1959.

About the Author

 Since completing his Ph.D. in 1977, Dr. Stanley E. Hibbs has practiced as a clinical psychologist in the Atlanta area. He has worked at community mental health centers, drug treatment programs, psychiatric hospitals, and he has taught at several local universities. His current private practice involves working with adolescents, adults, and couples.

For information, please contact Stanley E. Hibbs:

Phone: (770) 668-0350 X224
Fax: (770) 668-0417

E-mail: drhibbs@drhibbs.com
Web::   www.drhibbs.com

If you liked this book, you may be also interested in...

Corporate
Intelligence
Awareness

Securing the Competitive Edge

By Rodger Nevill Harding

Corporate Intelligence Awareness: Securing the Competitive Edge

In this compelling new book by a former diplomat, you will learn the secrets (step by step) to developing an intelligence strategy by effective information gathering and analyzing, and then to delivering credible intelligence to senior management. Along the way, you will learn how to better read people and organizations and get them to open up and share information with you—all the while behaving in an ethical, legal manner. Understanding how intelligence is gathered and processed will keep you ahead of the game, protect your secrets, and secure your competitive edge!

ISBN: 1-895186-42-0   (hardcover)
ISBN: 1-895186-43-9   (PDF ebook)

Also available in other ebook formats. Order from your local bookseller, Amazon.com, or directly from the publisher at
http://www.mmpubs.com/cia

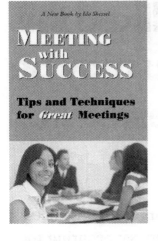

A New Book by Ida Shessel

MEETING
with
SUCCESS

Tips and Techniques
for *Great* **Meetings**

Are People Finding Your Meetings Unproductive and Boring?

Turn ordinary discussions into focused, energetic sessions that produce positive results.

If you are a meeting leader or a participant who is looking for ways to get more out of every meeting you lead or attend, then this book is for you. It's filled with practical tips and techniques to help you improve your meetings.

You'll learn to spot the common problems and complaints that spell meeting disaster, how people who are game players can effect your meeting, fool-proof methods to motivate and inspire, and templates that show you how to achieve results. Learn to cope with annoying meeting situations, including problematic participants, and run focused, productive meetings.

ISBN: 1-897326-15-7   (paperback)
Also available in ebook formats.

http://www.mmpubs.com/

Managing Smaller Projects:
A Practical Approach

So called "small projects" can have potentially alarming consequences if they go wrong, but their control is often left to chance. The solution is to adapt tried and tested project management techniques.

This book provides a low overhead, highly practical way of looking after small projects. It covers all the essential skills: from project start-up, to managing risk, quality and change, through to controlling the project with a simple control system. It cuts through the jargon of project management and provides a framework that is as useful to those lacking formal training, as it is to those who are skilled project managers and want to control smaller projects without the burden of bureaucracy.

Read this best-selling book from the U.K., now making its North American debut. *IEE Engineering Management* praises the book, noting that "Simply put, this book is about helping people control smaller projects in a logical and effective way, and making the process run smoothly, and is indeed a success in achieving that goal."

Available in print format. Order from your local bookseller, Amazon.com, or directly from the publisher at **www.mmpubs.com/msp**

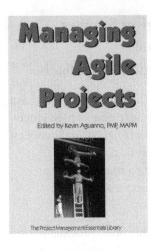

Edited by Kevin Aguanno, PMP, MAPM

The Project Management Essentials Library

Managing Agile Projects

Are you being asked to manage a project with unclear requirements, high levels of change, or a team using Extreme Programming or other Agile Methods?

If you are a project manager or team leader who is interested in learning the secrets of successfully controlling and delivering agile projects, then this is the book for you.

From learning how agile projects are different from traditional projects, to detailed guidance on a number of agile management techniques and how to introduce them onto your own projects, this book has the insider secrets from some of the industry experts – the visionaries who developed the agile methodologies in the first place.

ISBN: 1-895186-11-0   (paperback)
ISBN: 1-895186-12-9   (PDF ebook)

http://www.agilesecrets.com

Winston Churchill: The Agile Project Manager

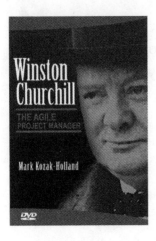

Today's pace of change has reached unprecedented levels only seen in times of war. As a result, project management has changed accordingly with the pressure to deliver and make things count quickly. This recording looks back at a period of incredible change and mines lessons for Project Managers today.

In May 1940, the United Kingdom (UK) was facing a dire situation, an imminent invasion. As the evacuation of Dunkirk unfolded, the scale of the disaster became apparent. The army abandoned 90% of its equipment, the RAF fighter losses were deplorable, and over 200 ships were lost.

Winston Churchill, one of the greatest leaders of the 20th century, was swept into power. With depleted forces and no organized defense, the situation required a near miracle. Churchill had to mobilize quickly and act with agility to assemble a defense. He had to make the right investment choices, deploy resources, and deliver a complete project in a fraction of the time. This recording looks at Churchill as an agile Project Manger, turning a disastrous situation into an unexpected victory.

ISBN: 1-895186-50-1   (Audio CD)
ISBN: 1-897326-38-6   (DVD)

http://www.PM-Audiobooks.com

Churchill's Adaptive Enterprise: Lessons for Business Today

This book analyzes a period of time from World War II when Winston Churchill, one of history's most famous leaders, faced near defeat for the British in the face of sustained German attacks. The book describes the strategies he used to overcome incredible odds and turn the tide on the impending invasion. The historical analysis is done through a modern business and information technology lens, describing Churchill's actions and strategy using modern business tools and techniques. Aimed at business executives, IT managers, and project managers, the book extracts learnings from Churchill's experiences that can be applied to business problems today. Particular themes in the book are knowledge management, information portals, adaptive enterprises, and organizational agility.

Eric Hoffer Book Award (2007) Winner

ISBN: 1-895186-19-6   (paperback)
ISBN: 1-895186-20-X   (PDF ebook)

http://www.mmpubs.com/churchill

Want to Get Ahead in Your Career?

Do you find yourself challenged by office politics, bad things happen-ing to good careers, dealing with the "big cheeses" at work, the need for effective networking skills, and keeping good working relation-ships with coworkers and bosses? *Winning the Rat Race at Work* is a unique book that provides you with case studies, interactive exercises, self-assessments, strategies, evaluations, and models for overcom-ing these workplace challenges. The book illustrates the stages of a career and the career choices that determine your future, empowering you to make positive changes.

Written by Peter R. Garber, the author of *100 Ways to Get on the Wrong Side of Your Boss*, this book is a must read for anyone interested in getting ahead in his or her career. You will want to keep a copy in your top desk drawer for ready reference whenever you find yourself in a challenging predica-ment at work.

ISBN: 1-895186-68-4   (paperback)
Also available in ebook formats. Order from your local bookseller, Amazon.com, or directly from the publisher at **http://www.mmpubs.com/rats**

100 Ways to Get on the Wrong Side of your Boss

And Strategies to Prevent you from Getting There !

Author of Winning the Rat Race at Work

Need More Help with the Politics at Work?

100 Ways To Get On The Wrong Side Of Your Boss (And Strategies to Prevent You from Getting There!) was written for anyone who has ever been frustrated by his or her working relationship with the boss—and who hasn't ever felt this way! Bosses play a critically important role in your career success and getting on the wrong side of this important individual in your working life is not a good thing.

Each of these 100 Ways is designed to illustrate a particular problem that you may encounter when dealing with your boss and then an effective strategy to prevent this problem from reoccurring. You will learn how to deal more effectively with your boss in this fun and practical book filled with invaluable advice that can be utilized every day at work.

Written by Peter R. Garber, the author of *Winning the Rat Race at Work*, this book is a must read for anyone interested in getting ahead. You will want to keep a copy in your top desk drawer for ready reference whenever you find yourself in a challenging predicament at work.

ISBN: 1-895186-98-6 (paperback)
Also available in ebook formats. Order from your local bookseller, Amazon.com, or directly from the publisher at
http://www.InTroubleAtWork.com

Networking *for* Results

In partnership with Michael J. Hughes, *The* Networking Guru, Multi-Media Publications Inc. has released a new series of books, ebooks, and audio books designed for business and sales professionals who want to get the most out of their networking events and help their career development.

Networking refers to the concept that each of us has a group or "network" of friends, associates and contacts as part of our on-going human activity that we can use to achieve certain objectives.

The *Networking for Results* series of products shows us how to think about networking strategically, and gives us step-by-step techniques for helping ourselves and those around us achieve our goals. By following these practices, we can greatly improve our personal networking effectiveness.

Visit **www.Networking-for-Results.com** for information on specific products in this series, to read free articles on networking skills, or to sign up for a free networking tips newsletter. Products are available from most book, ebook, and audiobook retailers, or directly from the publisher at **www.mmpubs.com**.

 **The Project Management Audio Library**

In a recent CEO survey, the leaders of today's largest corporations identified project management as the top skillset for tomorrow's leaders. In fact, many organizations place their top performers in project management roles to groom them for senior management positions. Project managers represent some of the busiest people around. They are the ones responsible for planning, executing, and controlling most major new business activities.

Expanding upon the successful *Project Management Essentials Library* series of print and electronic books, Multi-Media Publications has launched a new imprint called the *Project Management Audio Library*. Under this new imprint, MMP is publishing audiobooks and recorded seminars focused on professionals who manage individual projects, portfolios of projects, and strategic programmes. The series covers topics including agile project management, risk management, project closeout, interpersonal skills, and other related project management knowledge areas.

This is not going to be just the "same old stuff" on the critical path method, earned value, and resource levelling; rather, the series will have the latest tips and techniques from those who are at the cutting edge of project management research and real-world application.

www.PM-Audiobooks.com

CPSIA information can be obtained
at www.ICGtesting.com
Printed in the USA
BVHW042000120520
579550BV00009B/283